50 Abilities
Unlimited Possibilities
WHEELING THROUGH 50 STATES

From Jackson to the Boston Marathon Bombing

By Paul Erway

Praise for
Paul Erway and
50 Abilities, Unlimited Possibilities

"I am so proud of the accomplishments of these three guys. Not only have they been successful in bringing greater awareness to individuals living with Spinal Cord Injury, but also the mission of the Christopher & Dana Reeve Foundation. It's incredible what they have done and continue to do to help others."

Jill Farmer, CTRS, CDSS
Manager of Therapeutic Recreation, Frazier Rehabilitation

"Just when you thought your dreams were too big or too difficult, you find a book like Paul Erway's, which allows you to be inspired again! *50 Abilities, Unlimited Possibilities* is a story of overcoming obstacles and achieving big dreams, and serves as an inspiration for all of us! Thanks Paul, for sharing your story."

Cathy Fyock
Author, Book Coach

"Paul is my hero. His incredible life journey inspires a new kind of thinking for achieving one's potential through perseverance and self-belief. After reading this book, we all need to throw out any excuses not to reach for our dreams."

Cheryl Hart
Sport Psychology Consultant and Owner of 2nd Wind Motivation

"I raced with Grant and Paul in Ōita, Japan, where I first heard their plans about this challenge. I didn't think it could be done and they had to be crazy to try. This is true grit."

Matthew Porterfield
Fellow Wheelchair Athlete

50 Abilities
Unlimited Possibilities
WHEELING THROUGH 50 STATES

From Jackson to the Boston Marathon Bombing

By Paul Erway

50 Abilities, Unlimited Possibilities
Wheeling Through 50 States: From Jackson to the Boston Marathon Bombing
Book 1 of a 3-Book Series

Copyright © 2017 by Paul Erway
All rights reserved.

Published by Silver Tree Publishing, a division of
Silver Tree Communications, LLC (Kenosha, WI).

www.SilverTreeCommunications.com

*Throughout this book, the author shares amateur and professional photography taken
by family, friends, race supporters and others. Where applicable, attributions are
provided alongside such photos. In some instances, the author has been unable to iden-
tify the original photographer for an image placed in the public domain through social
media and, therefore, is unable to provide credit or detailed attribution.*

Editing by:
Duanne Puckett
Jeannette Buck
Jenny Smith
Kate Colbert

Cover design and typesetting by:
Courtney Hudson

Cover Photography by:
Sharrè Moore Myers, Plus2Studio

First print edition, October 2017

ISBN: 978-0-9991491-3-3

Library of Congress Control Number: 2017955812

Created in the United States of America

In Memory of:

Jimmy Green
Racer, Instructor, Mentor, Father, Husband, Friend
and Founder of Sportaid

Thank you for helping me and so many.

ACKNOWLEDGMENTS

I could not have taken on this immense type of a challenge alone so let me first thank Grant Berthiaume for having the faith that we could do this. 50 marathons in 50 states in 50 weeks! Grant's strength to not only pull through but to get each marathon accomplished in his fastest time will be an inspiration to all. Then there was his recruitment of Aaron Roux, a Marine who gave this journey character. I also received a lot of belief and support from Cheryl Hart, who kept guiding me from my second accident all the way to completion of this book and still remains a mentor to me.

Duanne Puckett and my Aunt Jeanette Buck helped with story-writing and early editing; I'm grateful also for their belief that I have a story to tell. My dad, Eugene Erway, and my seven siblings were so concerned for my health that they were pleading for me to stay with just a marathon a month, but ended up giving support in more ways than I could have wished for. There are so many friends and co-workers who I appreciate for the support they provided. Now to my wife, Barbara, who handled so much of home life while I was gone, even to the extent of full care of our six fur children. Thank you all.

Thank you to Amy Fountain, for support the day we presented at URC, and then support the day of the race, for the videos but best of all the photos she took, one of which was used on the 50 Abilities Marathon challenge promotions card.

I would like to give a special thanks to the generous organizations that provided underwriting support for this book: Coloplast, Permobil Cares, Sportaid, and Superior Van & Mobility.

And, finally, a thank you to my amazing publishing team at Silver Tree Publishing, Kate Colbert and Courtney Hudson, who worked long hours under an ambitious deadline to help me cross the "finish line" to make this book a reality. I couldn't have done it without them.

TABLE OF CONTENTS

Letter to the Reader   i

Foreword   v

Prologue   ix

Marathon #1   1
Jackson, Mississippi
    "Understanding"

Marathon #2   13
Houston, Texas
    "Leadership"

Marathon #3   23
Phoenix, Arizona
    "Enthusiasm"

Marathon #4   29
Miami, Florida
    "Inspirational"

Marathon #5   39
Myrtle Beach, South Carolina
　　　"Guidance"

Marathon #6   45
Birmingham, Alabama
　　　"Overcoming Fear"

Marathon #7   55
New Orleans, Louisiana
　　　"Gratitude"

Marathon #8   63
Albany, Georgia
　　　"Sweetness"

Marathon #9   69
Little Rock, Arkansas
　　　"Goal-Setting"

Marathon #10   75
Los Angeles, California
　　　"Flexible"

Marathon #11   83
Cape May, New Jersey
　　　"Open-Minded"

Marathon #12   91
Knoxville, Tennessee
　　　"Comradeship"

training session in my racing wheelchair while preparing for a marathon. This resulted in six weeks of hospitalization with four operations.

You may have heard the adage: "When you get thrown off a horse, you have to get right back in the saddle." In other words, you have to overcome your fear, you have to take control of the situation, and once you have done these two things, you will not believe the rides you can now take — the journey that you will experience.

Whenever you're faced with a difficulty, focus on the solution rather than on the problem. Think through the ideal solution to the obstacle rather than wasting time rehashing the problem. Solutions are inherently positive, whereas problems are inherently negative. The instant that you begin thinking in terms of solutions, you become a more positive and constructive human being.

I hope that you enjoy reading about my adventure on this fast-moving journey that was filled with fantastic people and unforeseen special moments. There were things that we did that were totally unexpected, that forced us to dig deep for strength to pull through, but there were also moments of pure enjoyments. In sharing these adventures, it is my desire to inspire you to get back in the saddle, overcome your fears, take control of your life and enjoy the journey.

Nearly everyone we talked to along our journey was telling us that we needed to write these stories down to make it into a book — that they were inspiring and so many need to know what we are going through. I was thinking "how hard can it be?" Two or three pages per marathon, times 50 marathons, throw in a few pictures, that will give us enough for a book. Right? So I started writing descriptions of each race, as well as the exciting things that happened around that event, which readers might enjoy. The problem was getting it all down on paper while still fresh in my memory. This started to become months and months of work because, at the same time, I was catching up on the many things I had to leave to

LETTER TO THE READER

Imagine the one thing you were passionate about when growing up. Was it soccer, baseball, or riding horses? Remember when you could not wait for school to be out so you could pursue what turns you on? Now, imagine you are in a terrible car accident with traumatic injuries and, within one second, all your dreams are taken away from you. How would you feel?

Similar experiences may haunt you, such as the unexpected death of a family member or spouse. Or your doctor calls after a routine screening test to say he wants to do further testing to rule out a suspicious tumor. How do you cope through these periods of anguish, getting yourself to face a life-altering event that forces you to change direction, to adapt, and to overcome?

Some life changes may not be as tragic, but at that moment they may appear that way to you. The storms of life batter everyone at some point. No matter how good a person you try to be, you're going to have some unexpected storms.

In my life, I have had two major events that changed and reshaped my life. The first was a car accident at age 21 that left me without the use of my legs. The second was 26 years later, when I hit a truck during a routine

Marathon #13   101
Adeline, Kansas
    "Hospitality"

Marathon #14   111
Boston, Massachusetts
    "Comprehend"

Epilogue   121

Resources   129

**Equipment and
Other Items Used**   137

the side for work and home, while still maintaining my full-time position. Then I began gathering photos, being sure I had the exact information. And being at the bottom percentage of English all through school, the task of writing a book was another huge challenge for me.

I would seek the guidance of other authors, finally connecting with Cathy Dorton Fyock who wrote On Your Mark: From First Word to First Draft in Six Weeks. I was informed that I had written three books, unless I drastically condensed the writing. I was told no one will want to read a book that thick; in today's society, no one's attention span is that long anymore. Plus no one will want to pay the amount of money it will cost to print an excessively long book. Harry Potter's story was not completed in one book; neither would the story of three guys wheeling through 50 states. I had to divide this challenge up. Each race had a story to tell, and each one had something that readers will want to know. I did not want to cut out some of the situations we faced, good or bad.

With Cathy Fyock's guidance, we decided to finish this book with the chapter on Boston, knowing it will be the most-read chapter. Boston was marathon #14 of 50. Because everyone in the United States was affected one way or another with this act of terrorism. Mark Zenobia, a source of consult for the Christopher & Dana Reeve Foundation (CDRF), brought new insight to the writing of this chapter. This will give the reader a taste of what we did to get started, some of the things we went through, and how tough it really is to take on such a challenge of completing 50 marathons in 50 states, all while trying to keep it in 50 weeks.

I hope you enjoy our adventure as much as we did.

FOREWORD

I feel a very personal connection to Paul Erway's story and the journey
he and his fellow wheelchair athletes embarked as they set out to race 50
marathons in 50 states over 50 weeks to raise awareness of spinal cord
injury. I am a marathoner myself and understand the intense prepara-
tion and dedication needed to persevere — and, in some cases, simply
survive. I am also the president and CEO of the Christopher & Dana
Reeve Foundation.

The mission of the Reeve Foundation is simultaneously simple and
extremely ambitious. We are dedicated to curing spinal cord injury by
funding innovative research and improving the quality of life for the
5.4 million Americans living with paralysis through grants, information and advocacy.

We fulfill this mission in a number of ways. We are leading the search
to find next-level therapies through research initiatives, such as the
International Research Consortium on Spinal Cord Injury and epidural
stimulation. And we put many of those therapies into practice at our
NeuroRecovery Network rehab facilities nationwide that promote
functional recovery and improve the health and overall quality of life for
people living with paralysis.

Through our Paralysis Resource Center — the primary source of information and support for people living with paralysis, their families and caregivers — we are often the recipients of the first call people make when a spinal cord injury occurs. Many times, we are the ones reaching out with trained information specialists who provide individualized information, help and hope.

Our Peer & Family Support Program, Quality of Life grants awarded to local nonprofits that mirror our mission, veterans' programs and advocacy work fulfill our dedication to fostering involvement in the community, promoting health and improving quality of life.

However, none of this is possible without funding. For this reason — and to foster the many thoughtful and proactive initiatives of so many caring individuals — we created Team Reeve (TeamReeve.org), our grassroots fundraising program. Team Reeve recruits and supports individuals or teams who want to run marathons, host local events or engage in opportunities to support the Reeve Foundation, its mission and people living with paralysis.

Team Reeve is a fixture at some of the most famed marathons in the country, including the TCS New York City Marathon and the Bank of America Chicago Marathon. These participants —runners, handcyclists and wheelchair racers alike — are extremely driven to not just complete the competitions but surpass their fundraising goals to propel research and develop life-changing treatments on behalf of the Reeve Foundation.

As you will discover throughout this book, Paul and his 50 Ability Marathon partners, Grant Berthiaume and Aaron Roux, bring this drive to a whole new level. Nothing about preparing for a marathon — training, pacing yourself during the race, figuring out transportation before and after the event — is easy.

Try doing that 50 times. Week after grueling week. In all 50 states. With a spinal cord injury, medical equipment and health considerations requiring constant attention. I can't begin to imagine the intense coordination involved.

On top of the complicated logistics and stamina required, these men aimed to visit hospitals and rehab facilities in each of the cities to spread their message about positivity and determination, as well as raise awareness for the Reeve Foundation. For people with spinal cord injury, perhaps no greater hope is offered than through the triumphant stories of those who came before them and conquered. It will be impossible to truly thank them for the immense effort, time and expense required to do this.

The hope and inspiration delivered, however, is mutual. It will become obvious to the readers of this book that, for Paul, Grant and Aaron, meeting with paralyzed individuals across the country didn't just bring considerable joy and broaden their perspectives on what it means to live with paralysis. It also encouraged them to continue their inimitable journey, further crystallizing the purpose of their mission to conquer all 50 races and raise funds for the paralysis community.

I also can't thank Paul enough for pushing this adventure further into the public sphere through this book. As I think of Paul and the journey he has endured, I can't help but think of Christopher Reeve. Like Christopher, who lived with a spinal cord injury for the rest of his life after being thrown from a horse in 1995, Paul was an equestrian. Like Christopher, Paul has remained positive about his situation and turned that attitude into something truly inspirational. And like Christopher, Paul is dedicated to giving back to the paralysis community in a very constructive way, seeking those cures that will inevitably prevail.

Through the efforts of people like Paul and his 50 Ability Marathon partners — role models for anybody looking to support an organization or cause — we are seeing dedicated individuals rallying to support the 1.3 million Americans living with a spinal cord injury and working tirelessly to develop therapies to improve their quality of life. From there, we will continue to make the steps and leaps necessary to get closer to Christopher Reeve's dream of a "world of empty wheelchairs."

Peter Wilderotter
President and CEO, Christopher & Dana Reeve Foundation

PROLOGUE

————

Let the story begin.

I was five when this love affair with horses began. I started horse shows at 11, trained my own at 16, and after high school, I went to college to study horses.

I did not do the traditional college route; I found an apprenticeship where I would stay at one of the top horse stables in the U.S. I would be out in the stable at 5:00 a.m. feeding the horses, riding by 6:00 a.m.; then I'd be off to classes, returning to ride until 10:00 or 11:00 p.m. and have all day on Saturdays and Sundays with the horses.

My view of passion is finding something that you would happily do without compensation regardless of the hours involved. This is something to reach for ... something that drives you beyond anything else in life.

What I experienced at this stable is what drove me to strive for excellence in their tack room. I was in awe of what I saw. There were countless trophies, ribbons with even prize saddles embossed with the date of the Championship that it had been won. From then on, I began applying more effort so that I, too, could be in the winner's circle.

It was the weekend of graduation from State University of New York in Morrisville. Our last weekend before reaching our goal in 1980, my best friend, Kevin, and I went on a double date with our girlfriends to commemorate what would likely be our last weekend to all be together.

I want to let you know, this was during the disco era, so get a picture of this kid 6'3", 160 pounds and on the dance floor with 3" platforms with a silk shirt doing his best John Travolta - Saturday Night Fever impersonation. It was epic. And on our journey toward home, on dark roads, our car ended up sliding into a ditch. In a construction site that had no markings. Even the stop sign had been taken down. The unfinished cleanup left loose gravel in the road, causing us to enter sideways into the ditch, which had also been left open. Seat belt laws had not yet been enacted.

In that instant, my horses were taken away.

The unthinkable had happened … and it had happened to me. I sustained a spinal cord injury (SCI) at the fourth thoracic vertebra (T4). I had been on the dance floor, showing off my best moves, and later that night, I became a paraplegic.

I completed my rehabilitation in what the medical experts called an extremely short time frame, but a lot of that was due to the support of great parents and seven siblings. Even on the day I was released, we did not go straight home. We went to dinner at a restaurant and then to a movie, like I was the same person just with better parking privileges.

Eight months after the accident, in January 1981, I returned to the same college in Morrisville, New York, to gain a business degree in hopes of managing a horse ranch. After a long snowy winter, excited for the first sunny spring day, I encountered the only other guy on campus who used a wheelchair, Mark. We pushed along toward the cafeteria when he says to me, "See that telephone pole? I'll race you to it."

This guy was half my size, skinny, with long scraggly curly hair, and a patchy eight-day beard. He was born with spina bifida, and he had never competed in any sports; he had never known how to train. Little did I realize he had used a wheelchair all his life; I only had 10 months' experience. So the 100-foot distance was nothing for him. He beat me by half the distance. I looked around to see if anyone had witnessed my defeat.

That started the fire to burn in me. If I'm going to be in a wheelchair, I'm going to train to see how fast I can push it. Then I will come back and crush this little guy.

I got back in the saddle. But now I call it my "chrome pony."

I did get into wheelchair racing (from regional track to Nationals then the World Championships in Assen, Holland, in 1990), which has so many stories that could fill its own book. I have had the opportunity to meet some great people along the way, one of whom is Grant Berthiaume.

Grant Berthiaume was working construction on one of those sunny days in which you think nothing could go wrong. He was up on a roof, acting a little too easy with the dangers of his position, and maybe a little too close to the edge. In that instant, his fall crushed his 10th thoracic vertebra. He had to find the way to pick himself up. As with me, we found something to reach for … something that gave us a chance to compete in the game of life. And that was wheelchair racing.

We both have completed the Boston Marathon several times. As everyone knows, it is the greatest marathon in the United States. Oh, by the way, they do have a racing wheelchair division. But only in the last couple of years have they really recognized this division and given a little bit of coverage on TV.

The greatest marathon for racing wheelchairs, though, is Ōita, Japan. It is strictly for racing wheelchairs. There are no runners at all in this race.

Once you get to Japan, they take care of the rest of your travel. They pay for four nights in a hotel, along with the breakfast. Everyone is out for the rest of the meals, exploring the city and all that it has to offer culturally.

———

Pushing Further

Grant and I were in our shared room in Ōita and we asked each other, "What's next?" We had accomplished the greatest marathon in the United States when we did Boston. We had just completed the greatest wheelchair race in the world by competing in Ōita, Japan.

Grant said, "You know, marathon runners try to do a marathon in every state. There is a 50 States Club that we could join. And who knows, we may be the first wheelchair racers to ever do that!"

"If there are 50 states and 52 weeks in a year, what if we did the 50 marathons in 50 states in 50 weeks? Wouldn't that be something?" I said.

Two months later, Grant calls me up and says, "Hey, we can do it!"

During our planning, Grant said, "There is this guy in Tucson who has pushed his hand-cycle from California to Florida in 60 days. If a guy like that can accomplish something that big, we need him on our team." Hand-cycling is like a recumbent bike with 27 gears, whereas our racing chairs only have push rims. Thus, our connection to Aaron Roux.

Aaron Roux was in the Marines and was deployed for two tours overseas. He was home for a week of rest before returning for another tour of duty. In Michigan, in December, he was out with his buddies, not drinking, but a snow storm caused the car to slide off the road. The telephone pole that they hit came crashing down on the passenger side, right where Aaron was sitting. He had a fracture at the seventh cervical vertebra, meaning he became a quadriplegic (quad) with all four limbs affected – his legs and hands. His injury is higher than mine by five vertebrae. I am a paraplegic (para) meaning two, in which my two limbs, my legs, are the ones affected by paralysis. I have more muscle control than Aaron, but he is strong enough to get up from the floor into his wheelchair faster than I can. This guy is amazing. He was a great addition to our team with his strength and the determination of a Marine.

———

Reason Why

We did realize this would be a serious challenge. No wheelchair athlete had ever done this before, so we needed an even bigger reason to do it … a reason to motivate us when it got so tough we were tempted to quit. But we couldn't, because we weren't doing this for us. It was for the people we want to help. Wouldn't it be grand if we could raise money for spinal cord injury (SCI) research to help find a cure?

I had known about the Christopher & Dana Reeve Foundation (CDRF) and all that they were doing for SCI. I told Grant of the sign on the wall in the therapy gym where Christopher Reeve did his rehab. It was so fitting for what we wanted to accomplish.

> *"For everyone who thought I couldn't do it,*
> *For everyone who thought I shouldn't do it,*

For everyone who said I didn't have it in me,
See you at the finish line."

— TeamReeve.org —

Thus, we set out to do 50 marathons in 50 states in 50 weeks. Each marathon, each state has a story, but it is also the "Behind the Scenes" with each race that I think you will find interesting. There were challenges we experienced within this challenge. The exciting people we met. Things that we got to do, which were not planned. Each chapter has its own story to tell. I invite you to enjoy them all.

But what I really hope you gain from this is a new way to face your own challenges. When you are hit with a circumstance that leaves you thinking "there is no way past this" or when you are having a bad time with something, my fellow racers and I hope you can reflect back to this book and say: "If these three guys can do this, in that race, or that situation, after all that they went through, and have such a fantastic journey along the way, I, too, need to find my race to run."

MARATHON #1
Jackson, Mississippi

"Understanding"

———

January 5, 2013
7:00 a.m.

"The best-laid schemes of Mice and Men oft go awry,
And leave us nothing but grief and pain.
For promised joy!"

— Robert Burns —

A quote by Robert Burns seems appropriate for the first leg of our 50 marathons challenge. Our 50-marathon challenge began in Jackson, Mississippi. In order for me to get there, I had to drive 618 miles, while Grant and Aaron flew the 1,327 miles from Arizona to join me. This would be our first official meeting in person. Despite the hours of communication via phone or emails, we still had work to do for the upcoming year. What we did know was that we had a common cause: Our goal was to bring awareness that a person could have a fulfilled life even after a life-changing circumstance.

Before we started our race, there was the presentation we agreed to do for University Rehabilitation Center.

University Rehabilitation Center at the University of Mississippi

But with little time, we had to scramble in an attempt to look like we were organized to have something to hand out at our presentation. We found an instant printer shop. After a short conversation there, we determined that a small postcard would be ideal to contain contact information yet be easy enough to carry. We would hand this out to anyone asking who we were and what we were doing. It was a great idea, but without a photo of the three of us together, we would not have the postcards ready for our initial presentation. Thus, we put this project on the list for our next event.

Just push forward anyway.

We were well aware that not every plan rolls along smoothly. There were going to be bumps along the way. There would be mental and physical pain to endure. But there would be the joy of accomplishing our goal in the end.

The tension started to build as we hurriedly began to prepare as best as we could in the half hour before loading into the minivan. We discussed

the order in which we would speak and what information needed
to be presented.

As we were pulling up to the back side of University Rehabilitation
Center's parking lot, we saw the person with whom we had made the
arrangements. There was a look of concern as he stared at his cell phone.
We wondered if he was having second thoughts about allowing us to
speak, seeing as we hadn't even raced the first marathon but were confi-
dently proclaiming that we were going to complete 50!

Although we had arrived at the appointed time, there was one television
crew that had showed up early. Their goal was to get an interview before
we began our presentation. This interview would have to wait as the
staff had already lined up most of the patients, plus we had to set up our
screen and projector to show our website. We did have my six-year-old
racing wheelchair, the cleanest one of the bunch, to give our audience an
idea of what equipment we used in racing.

Our audience was a combination of administrative staff, therapists,
patients, and two news crews from local television stations. After our
presentation, there was an awkward silence. No one had any questions.
Luckily, the television crew still wanted that interview. This helped fill the
quiet in the room. Afterward, we exchanged a few handshakes with the
attendees and answered a few questions from those who had not wanted
to ask in front of the rest of the audience.

The key staff members at the center then took the three of us to
lunch. We felt relieved that we had completed the presentation.
Isn't everyone's biggest fear speaking in front of a group of people?
The considerable benefit of this luncheon was it provided us with an
opportune moment to discuss our ideas and how we could improve
on presenting our message for future audiences. Our conversation
included our ideas to help them, if they would want to start an adaptive
sports program.

The best part from the race in Jackson was the moment after our presentation at the rehab center when we learned that there were some moved by our message … one quad wanted to find out about playing Quad Rugby and another was interested in wheelchair basketball and how he could start racing. This gave us the UNDERSTANDING of why we were there and that we do have a message to help others when we speak from the heart.

Because this was our first race, we wanted to be sure things went well. So after the lunch, we decided to travel the course ahead of time, giving us an idea of what was to come. The race director had warned us that the course would be challenging with all the hills and rough roads. But it had never stopped any wheelchair racers from competing in the past.

It was a good thing that we decided to do this. Or was it?

When racers check out a course map, they usually find, in most cases, an elevation chart. This one did not show any flat spots; either you were going up a hill or going down one. As we started driving, there were no flat spots in the course at all and the roads were very rough. Worse than we anticipated. We were even driving at a slow rate so we could pick and choose through this maze of road to find the smoothest route to take. We had only gotten 10 miles into this drive when we got so depressed that we turned back with the hope that it all can't be that bad. We would not find out until we were actually out there and committed to complete the race to see if the rest of the course was actually that rough. What a bitter pill we had to swallow to complete this race!

The bright spot in the gloom was that we were able to obtain hotel rooms within blocks of the start/finish line of the marathon. This allowed us to get into our racing chairs in the hotel lobby. The staff would place our everyday chair at a secured location until our return.

I also noted the weather. It was much warmer in the lobby than outside and — as we would find it to be true in future races — I also have to mention how nice it is when hotels have those automatic doors that open wide as you get close to them. A true blessing since we were tucked into our chairs with racing gloves on.

As it turned out, we found we had made a positive impression with the audience at the rehabilitation center. On the morning of the race, the three of us were happily surprised when a therapist, Amy Fountain, from University Rehabilitation Center appeared. This thoughtful therapist offered to help us in any way she could. This was a very generous offer, especially as it was only 34 degrees that morning.

With Amy Fountain from the University Rehabilitation Center

When Grant investigated this race in Jackson, he saw that someone had completed it last year in 2:40 (2 hours, 40 minutes). That did not bother Grant one bit; he finished the Boston Marathon in 1:40.

But now as we came up to the starting line, there was a younger guy from the University of Illinois. That was not an encouraging thing. You see, anyone attending that college is probably a very good racer unless it is their first month of college. The coaching staff there is among the top in the nation to get students, as we say, "up to speed."

I knew Grant liked to stay "up to speed" with his competition. And before every race he'd say, "Put the hammer down."

I'd like to provide everyone with a little insight into Grant and his competitiveness. He does not like to take second place. Not even to the runners. This tendency would show itself numerous times over the course of the year and we saw this right away on this very first race day. We had discussed before the race, between the three of us, that for most of the race we would try to stay together. But when we arrived at the start line and Grant saw the competition, he was off with the starter's gun. There went any plans for staying together.

Can you imagine the emotions we were feeling at the starting line? More than two years of planning, trying to find sponsorship, the logistics of not only this race, but the plans for the next eight as these weeks will start to fly by. I also had my regular position to work during the week as well, but here we are ready for the first one. No wonder Grant shot out of there like he was actually in the starting gun.

Aaron and I attempted to stay together for the first six miles. Nevertheless, I could climb hills better, while Aaron could fly on the downhill. We were back and forth until I found the lack of training for this first marathon, as well as the rough roads, were taking its toll on me. We also realized that the rough, elevated course we saw the day we drove the first 10 miles was the carbon-copy of the last 16.2 miles. We were going up steep, very long hills, and then down even shorter ones with very little rest before we had to begin climbing again, amidst potholes galore.

Yet, we all appreciated the crowd cheering us on as we came close to the end. I was thinking, Not much farther, just up this hill. Then I heard someone say, "It is just around this corner!" only to find the finish line was actually around the corner and uphill three more blocks!

Grant finished second behind a racer half his age. Aaron took fourth and I finished in fifth place. Grant had waited for Aaron and me, along with Amy, who was being so supportive by taking photos and video at the finish. We wanted to commemorate our first race of 50. Amy even helped transport Grant's and Aaron's racing chairs back to the airport. This was so kind of her.

Grant is a veteran at marathons, having about 50 already under his belt in the previous nine years.

"This is the toughest marathon I have ever done," he said. "And this is great that it is our first, for the rest will be easy compared to this one."

I was hoping Grant was right. After that first marathon, I jotted, "I am hurting and still have a nine-and-a-half-hour drive left to get home and I still need to be at work at 8 o'clock Monday morning." The duration of driving gave me time to reflect on this past weekend, with sharpened perception for the coming weeks.

In the end, our presentation at the rehab center was the most inspiring part of our first marathon today. When we got home, we received this note via email:

Aaron, Grant, Paul —

Thanks for coming to Mississippi! You truly were an encouragement to our patients and our staff at University Rehab!

Now we have two guys (one para, one quad) who are very interested in trying out wheelchair sports, thanks to you! You gave the therapists and nurses a renewed enthusiasm for helping the patients achieve their highest potentials. Everyone will be talking about you all for a while!

Below are links for your story in Mississippi publications — thanks for inspiring people throughout the state! … Best wishes for a year of great races! Hopefully they'll all be easy after the MS Blues Marathon! We at URC will keep following your story and praying for your safety & success!

Amy Fountain

RACE RESULTS
(position, time, name, age)

1st (02:02:28) – James Senbeta, 26

2nd (02:24:08) – Grant Berthiaume, 51

3rd (02:42:58) – John Payne, 33

4th (03:15:59) – Aaron Roux, 28

5th (03:25:25) – Paul Erway, 54

Celebrating at the Finish Line

Behind the Scenes

The posse discussed dining out on Friday night in a new town — the first pre-race meal of many to come. We did not want to wind up in any chains or places that we had undertaken before, but to experience the atmosphere of the town, state, or culture we were in.

The hotel staff recommended three places. The first one did not work.

As we approached, we found, as is too often still the case, that the restaurant was not wheelchair accessible due to the age of the building. Nor had they made any renovations that would bring it up to code to meet ADA standards. But this turned out to be a situation that happens to us all too often and we had to compromise many times over the course of the year as we found restaurants and other buildings inaccessible.

The second one was a grand choice, for it had an added bonus: A very lovely lady also approached the door and graciously held it open for us.

As we waited inside for our table, we asked (because she appeared to be in great shape) if she was in town for the marathon. She said yes and asked if we are doing the same. Since Grant and Aaron are both single, they asked if she was expecting someone to dine with her. To their joy, she was alone and would be glad to join us.

Her name was Becky and she was planning to run the half marathon the following day.

It is a small world, at times. Her mission was to run a half marathon every weekend for 52 weeks, wherever she can find one in her traveling work area. How great is that? After comparing our schedules, it appeared that we would very likely be crossing paths again.

One of the joys in doing all of these events is to be able to meet interesting people and to hear their stories.

Becky explained that she dresses in a different outfit every race, had no time limit to finishing the race, simply "does each one of them for the enjoyment of staying healthy, meeting new people, and adding excitement to her business travel." She does not have any sponsors, but because her husband also travels so much, she uses his frequent flyer miles and hotel discounts.

Can you imagine what is going through our mind at the starting line of the first of 50 marathons? And then she comes up to wish us well with her attire for the race — dressed like she's going to a costume party instead of a marathon. What a fun attitude for life!

Sometimes you just need to reach out to someone you don't know. In this case, it was just being nice since it is not always the best time eating alone. And who knows who they are and how much they will touch your life? This was a true blessing meeting her, while putting a sizable smile on our face!

————

Possibilities

"A goal should scare you a little, and excite you a lot."

— Joe Vitale —

MARATHON #2
Houston, Texas

"Leadership"

January 13, 2013
7:00 a.m.

Because of Grant's experience with racing marathons, we followed his lead. He showed us LEADERSHIP as he explained that after the first grueling race, the rest would be a piece of cake. He took over providing expectations and the entire year's schedule. Throughout the project, though, we then did try to share some of these responsibilities.

With his experience, Grant called the first race of this challenge "the toughest marathon we will do all year." We were really looking forward to this second race. Grant had raced the Houston Marathon before. And he assured us it was pretty flat with much smoother roads (because most are cement) than the previous one. The seven-day weather forecast showed 70 degrees and sunny. Now how can you beat that? A chance to be warm for a race — in January! It's always warm in Texas, right?

I flew into Texas Thursday night after work because the time difference was to my advantage. In true Texas style, our host — a therapist — picked me up the next morning in her pickup truck. If you're going to be in Texas, you have to ride in a pickup. As it happened, the therapist had met Aaron two years prior when he hand-cycled from California to

Florida in 64 days. This is one of the reasons Grant wanted Aaron on our team. Grant knew this guy had the determination and guts to make it through all of the races.

As had been the case in Jackson, we began our experience in Houston by speaking at a rehab center. I had heard of the TIRR Memorial Hermann's rehabilitation center from Kim Atkinson, who is Director of Spinal Cord Medicine at Frazier Rehab in Louisville, Kentucky. Kim and her husband had both worked at TIRR Memorial Hermann before they had moved to Kentucky to work with Frazier Rehab, as both facilities are supported by the Christopher & Dana Reeve Foundation (CDRF).

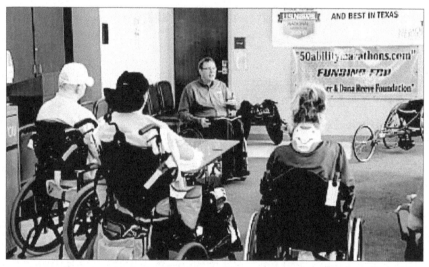

TIRR Memorial Hermann Rehabilitation Center

So my anticipation was high, for this would be the first presentation with the patients that I would deliver alone, while Grant and Aaron were still traveling in. They would be there to help with the second presentation, which was with all the therapists and staff.

Little did I realize that there would also be two TV stations there for the first presentation. Remember, this was only my second presentation, and this time, I was going it alone without my fellow racers for their input, and we had completed just one race of 50. But it actually worked very well that the first presentation was for the patients and for the TV crew. I was speaking to the patients from my heart about being in two accidents. Then I spoke of Grant's and Aaron's stories. Then I built up to what created this challenge. The other two arrived in time for the staff and therapist presentation.

We focused on thanking the therapists for encouraging people with paralysis to take on challenges without being afraid to move forward with their disability. They can have amazing adventures. They have the choice to write their own story with the whole facility's support.

At the Fitness Expo

Saturday was filled with a fitness expo and with picking up our race numbers, as well as trying to make connections for possible sponsorships. Well, at least I was looking for sponsorships. We did not know that Aaron is quite the shopper when he gets that close to athletic gear, so, yes, we spent a lot of time at the expo!

When we came into the exhibit hall, the wonderful smells from the food court made us eager to grab a quick bite. While we were sitting there, a very quiet, petite blonde holding a microphone came up to Grant, who wore a sleeveless shirt that showed off his enormous arms. He is like a magnet for women. They always come up to him.

"Are you doing the race tomorrow?" she asked. His face lit up with a big smile and he took the opportunity to give his two-minute pitch of the 50 Ability Marathons, the name we had given our challenge. She was a television reporter sent out to capture something about this marathon. With her cameraman, she began following us and we continued filling her in as we went to pick up our race numbers. The crowd began staring at us, wondering who these three guys using wheelchairs were and why the TV crew was chasing them. Each of us did a personal interview in the hallway in front of a large race banner. After all of this, though, the news broadcast that night only gave us about one minute of coverage.

At the expo, we heard rumors of a cold front rapidly moving into the area, which could arrive during the night and bring lots of rain. The TV stations, however, were saying that this front could slow down and not arrive until later. We learned afterward, by way of rumor, that the television stations were stretching that tale in hopes of bringing more people downtown for this event.

Again, we lucked out with our hotel being just a few blocks from the start and finish lines. As my excitement was building, I transferred into my racing chair inside the nice warm lobby as we anticipated improved racing conditions. I am used to the Eastern time zone, so the 5:00 a.m. wakeup call was my chance to sleep to 6:00 a.m. But for Grant and Aaron, this was an early 4:00 a.m.

Upon exiting the hotel, we glanced at each other in dismay for what greeted us. Hidden from the dark, early morning was not the warm, dry weather we were expecting. Rather the cold front truly moved in with its bleak temperature and light rain now coming down on us, with the gloom of cloudiness making it worse.

In addition to ourselves, there were only four other wheelchair racers, which is uncommon for such a great marathon. But local racers weren't committed with a challenge like ours, nor had they already invested the time and travel we had. So who would blame them for not putting themselves through this situation? We were unprepared for this turn of events.

At the Houston Marathon Starting Line

While we were waiting at the start line, the clouds opened. A bitter cold rain poured down, drenching us. Weeks later, we found a photo of the three of us sitting in the dark rain, illuminated only by a street light. My head was down as if I was praying that the rain might stop or at least ease off so we could have a safe ride.

It helped that the local bicycle club volunteered to ride alongside us, as fewer wheelchair racers were on hand to start and the fact that we started just minutes ahead of the runners meant we spread out quickly. Bike companions can be a great safety precaution, especially at intersections. We're very cautious because we are so low to the ground and have sometimes been overlooked by cross-traffic.

My bike companion, who was a new guy to riding this race, really did not know the course. However, he did become a very valuable asset, as you'll see in "Behind the Scenes."

The first three-quarters of a mile, Aaron and I were just trying to get traction on the push rims with such heavy rain coming down. Then we started up the overpass. This was a pretty flat course, but that is after you do this half-mile hill climb. True to form, Grant was gone with the word Go, giving in to his competitive spirit to beat other wheelchair racers who were about his speed. Aaron was ahead of me until halfway up this first climb, when I pushed harder to get to the top with as much distance as I could muster. I assumed in a really tight tuck to decrease wind resistance on the downside, trying to stay in front of Aaron as long as I could.

My unsure companion on the bike went the wrong way at the fork in the road. Oh, no!

Doubling back as we corrected my course, there was Aaron waving goodbye, still having a great coast off the hill, which I hate to miss out on as they are my favorite part of any race.

When the race was over, I met up with Grant at the hotel. We were both surprised that Aaron was not back, because we knew he was ahead of me. There was no answer on his cell phone. He returned our call half an hour later saying he had been taken to the medical tent a mere mile away. We started wheeling over there in our dry, everyday clothes as the rain had stopped by then.

Because Aaron has a higher-level spinal cord injury, he is more susceptible to hyperthermia. We learned that at the 25-mile mark of the race, he had been weaving back and forth in a peculiar manner. Someone had taken him to the medical tent. His temperature was so low, it could not be read. The people there stripped off his clothes, hung them to dry, put him on a table with heated blankets, and gave him warm liquids. After an hour, his temperature was back up, close to what it should be. Once dressed in dry clothes, this former Marine insisted on finishing the race. With it no longer raining and a strong tailwind for the last mile, he was able to complete the race, showing his undaunted determination.

RACE RESULTS

1st (02:12:29) – Grant Berthiaume

3rd (04:48:15) – Aaron Roux

Paul Erway – DNF (did not finish)

Behind the Scenes

Thanksgiving 2012: I always enjoy our annual family get together in Ocean City, Maryland. It's quite a large affair, as I am one of eight siblings, their spouses and lots of kids. This week, the weather for that area was actually nice enough for golfing, biking, and beach combing. It worked out well that my father, 85 years old, had connections at the local golf club because he still was employed there part-time, keeping his green thumbs dirty. You just can't keep a good man down. But he says he likes to see dazzling plants and flowers as he golfs in the afternoons.

We gorged ourselves with the customary Thanksgiving feast on Thursday, a theme party on Friday night, after which we open our exchange

Christmas gifts. Our final event is the breakfast buffet Saturday at the golf clubhouse.

What I didn't expect was to be the focus of the family's concerns for my age and well-being. I was finishing my second plate, ready to push away from the table, when my other siblings moved into the seats around the table. Their plan was to talk me out of doing the 50-marathon challenge. I reminded them that in the previous six weeks, I had completed three marathons to test myself to be sure I was up for this challenge. At the last one, I finished fast enough to qualify for the Boston Marathon in the spring of 2013. The family discussed with me the idea of only doing one marathon a month, while letting the other two guys get all 50 marathons. They returned home happy with their agreement. Needless to say, deep down inside, this provided another gear to shift into proving myself to overcome any obstacle.

Houston Texas 2013: Week two and my second marathon, I got a flat tire on my right disc wheel in the vicinity of mile six. After 30 years of racing, this is nothing new. The down side is changing the tire while sitting in the racing chair. People see your situation and want to help, but we sometimes spend more time educating them on the product than it would take if we did it ourselves. When I showed my displeasure in getting a flat, the bike companion, who I mentioned earlier in the chapter, proved to be beneficial. Ryan, who owns Bicycle World of Houston, had plenty of experience in changing this type of tire.

Let me describe this disc wheel. It uses a vibration-absorbing material sandwiched between layers of rigid carbon laminate attached to the wheel rim. When the wheel receives an impact from the road, much of the shock is absorbed. They use a Kevlar® thread to bind these sheets of carbon to each other. Because Kevlar is 350% more impact-resistant than carbon, it can disperse shock more evenly throughout the carbon laminate, making a strong wheel rim. The surface is dimpled like a golf ball, or as the manufacturer says, "Aerodynamic Advanced Boundary." This refers to the patented and instantly recognizable dimpled pattern found on all of their carbon rims. It allows air to flow across the rim's surface with less resistance. In other words, these are unquestionably one of the reasons a racing wheelchair is expensive.

One does not want to wheel with a flat tire for very long, because of the risk of tearing up the discs and having to buy a new one. The tires on these discs are called "sew up." Literally, it is a rubber tube with a piece of cloth sewn over it with a scant amount of tread melted on. This makes for a very lightweight tire — and one that is very easy to change. You just peel it off and then put a little bit of glue on the rim, stretching the new tire on. Then with CO_2 we inflate the tire in seconds and are back in the race with little more than a couple minutes' down time.

Thus, with Ryan's help changing the tire, in record time I was back wheeling again in the race.

Then another problem arose. In those 30 years of racing, I had never gotten more than one flat in one race. So, to save weight on my chair for 26.2 miles, I — and the other two racers — had only carried one spare. Coming up to mile 11, I got another flat tire on the same side. And, of course, I was without a spare. Being the last guy, the bike rider Ryan can't stop one of the other wheelers to borrow one. I had to make a decision. I could still push to see how long the disc would last, knowing I would be buying a new one at a hefty price. Or should I give into my family's wish that I not try to kill myself? For the first time in very long time, I realized my day was done. Or as runners know what is recorded on the books: DNF (did not finish). This was one of the reasons we were doing this challenge as a team, as situations like this come up for us that runners don't have to deal with.

From this race forward, all three of us carried two spare tires and two CO_2 cartridges to resolve this for the rest of the challenge. It was a key learning experience that would be used many more times in the coming year.

––––––––

Possibilities

"Every adversity, every failure, every heartache carries with it the seed on an equal or greater benefit."

— Napoleon Hill —

MARATHON #3
Phoenix, Arizona

"Enthusiasm"

———

January 20, 2013
7:00 a.m.

Looking through this chapter, you will find various descriptive phrases that show why ENTHUSIASM pushed us along, race after race, state after state. Great interaction. Fantastic run. Smooth and straight roads. Warm and sunny. Enjoyable entertainment. And experienced volunteers and staff.

We made arrangements to speak at Barrow Neurological Institute before the third marathon. As luck would have it, our timing was a bit off. Program Coordinator Jo Crawford's hands were tied. Just two days before we were to speak, six patients with spinal cord injury had been discharged. This was our key target audience. We know from experience, once a patient gets out, he or she simply doesn't want to go back to a hospital, no matter who is scheduled to present. Then there was the Joint Commission for the Facilities Accreditation, who made their yearly unannounced visit. This puts the whole staff on pins and needles. The only patients they could rustle up to hear us were not the most enthusiastic about being at the facility, let alone interested hearing some crazy guys talk about racing wheelchairs in weekly marathons. Some of them knew nothing about marathons. The few therapists who did come made it all worthwhile and we enjoyed their great interaction with us. It was helpful that they already knew Grant and Aaron as the local guys doing wheelchair sports.

This was going to be one fantastic run being in Grant and Aaron's backyard, so to speak. I had even done this race twice before and I truly enjoyed the course. All of us always looked forward to racing in Phoenix.

My brother Dana and his wife Ginger lived in the area, and they had coaxed me to go out there the first time. But just hearing how warm and sunny it is in January was enticement enough.

Now to the course itself. The first half looks flat, but don't let that fool you. There is a slight incline. But here comes the best part — the second half changes to a gentle downhill and one can really pick up the pace. The roads were mostly straight, as well as smooth. And have I told you how warm and sunny it is?

The other great factor in choosing this race was that it was one of the Rock 'n' Roll series of races. This organization holds various races throughout the United States. As the name implies, they enlist local bands or DJs along the route to entertain and keep the miles passing by. There was just about every type of music imaginable, including high school bands and cheerleaders. There might have even be a local drum corps, loud enough to hear coming and going for quite a distance.

The best part for us in this particular Rock 'n' Roll event was that they had a designated staff person for the wheelchair division. Her name was Jennifer Nanista. Jennifer had been with this organization for a long time and she knew how to organize and be very helpful to the wheelchair athletes. She had become a friend to us, for this was not the only Rock 'n' Roll race that we entered. She had gotten to know us and our 50 Ability

At the Phoenix Marathon Starting Line

Marathons as we relied on her knowledge while we were organizing the challenge. That actuality played a significant role in assisting us later in the year at another event.

Jennifer had our packets ready to pick up in a separate area away from the masses at their race expo. And she gave us VIP parking passes near the starting line. There was a local bicyclist club and Jennifer made arrangements to have a cyclist with each wheelchair racer to help them stay the course and be of support if there was equipment failure. This was very reassuring for us.

They were also great at handling our everyday chairs, which were taken from the start to the finish line because the race was a point-to-point event. At the finish, we were given VIP passes to a tent area so it was easy to find our everyday chairs — again away from the masses. The food was also great — better than the average runner received.

A very strong contingent of hand-cyclists enjoys this race because the Wounded Veterans organization is very prominent in this area and are there to help out. We highly recommend this marathon, not only for the wheelchair division, but for runners as well. Have I told you how sunny and warm it is there in January?

At the Finish Line

RACE RESULTS

Ten wheelers participated in the Wheelchair Division.

3rd (02:02:37) – Grant Berthiaume

8th (02:32:48) – Aaron Roux

9th (02:36:31) – Paul Erway

Behind the Scenes

The major sponsor of the event was PF Chang's restaurant. The first year I did this race, I had heard of this restaurant chain but had never eaten in one. After I picked up my race packet with my brother, who had come to help me out with transportation, we spotted one nearby and decided that if they put up that kind of money for this big of an event, there must be something to their food. There is. The food is healthy with lots of choices and the staff is friendly.

My brother and I looked at each other and said, "You know, it is a grand place to eat."

We hope they continue to sponsor that event, with prayers that they expand to all of the races. PF Chang's has made us a big fan and frequenter of their establishments — all because of their sponsorship.

Possibilities

"The secret of health for both mind and body is not to mourn for the past, not to worry about the future, or not to anticipate troubles, but to live in the present moment wisely and earnestly."

— Buddha —

MARATHON #4
Miami, Florida

"Inspirational"

January 27, 2013
6:15 a.m.

Meeting Sabrina Cohen, who made it her mission to help other individuals with a disability improve their fitness and quality of life, was INSPIRATIONAL. This is what inspired us with our endeavor — such chance meetings with people like Sabrina. We are united in the hope of finding a cure that would help so many others. One of her future goals is to make the beaches of Miami accessible to those unable to navigate the sand in the usual manner.

On Sunday, January 27, 2013, the race began at 6:15 a.m. in front of the American Airlines Arena, 601 Biscayne Blvd. This was the 11th running of this race. With a record of more than 25,000 participants, it was one of the top five marathons in the country. The race was sponsored by ING, the global financial institution of Dutch origin. This was also our first meeting with the organization Achilles International. Their mission is "To enable people with all types of disabilities to participate in mainstream athletics in order to promote personal achievement, enhance self-esteem, and lower barriers to living a fulfilled life."

Our Miami weekend began on Friday with a speaking engagement with Miami Physical Therapy Associates Inc. Thus, contacting the National Mobility Equipment Dealers Association (NMEDA), I was able to ensure that Auto Mobility Sales was our best choice to arrange a wheelchair-accessible rental van.

Having arrived on different flights, we gathered our gear and contacted the hotel shuttle service. Despite their rapid appearance, the large transport vehicle was not wheelchair-accessible. Their terminology was that their shuttle was "accommodating," meaning the driver is very strong and could lift us up into the bus. Despite this encounter, the friendly and helpful driver got us to the hotel safe and sound.

We were able to secure our weekend transportation needs through the National Mobility Dealers Association. Their ultimate mission is to unify and improve the mobility equipment industry and help people with disabilities lead happy, healthy and more mobile lifestyles through the use of quality wheelchair accessible vehicles. This does not have anything to do with making sure hotels meet ADA rules and regulations, but with their dealer network they helped us find Auto Mobility Sales of Miami. Once they heard our tale of what we wanted to do, they contributed a wheelchair-accessible Dodge Grand Caravan for us to use. I should add that they even had it to the hotel before we arrived and after the weekend was over, they picked it back up for us. Great customer service is not dead, as some might believe.

The trick now was figuring out how three guys with three everyday wheelchairs and three racing wheelchairs would fit into the vehicle for all of the weekend's travel. Then on Sunday, after all that practice, we still had to squeeze our luggage in with us when we returned to the airport.

Once unpacked in the room, we ventured out to a resplendent day in Miami. We wanted to explore the area, thus getting to our appointment early. This turned into a great unexpected benefit. Just across the street from the Miami Physical Therapy Association, we noticed a restaurant that was about to open and it was a great dining experience. Then and there we vowed to not eat at any chain places, but experience local cuisine whenever we could during this challenge for the rest of the year.

When we went back across the street for our presentation, we found that the Miami Physical Therapy staff had a pizza feast awaiting, thinking we would be carb-loading for the marathon.

Meeting Sabrina Cohen at the facility while meeting the staff where she had completed her rehab after being injured was inspirational. It was powerful just knowing they were instrumental in her becoming one of those great people who moved forward in life, giving her strength in mentoring others through the recovery. These are the places that truly care for the sustenance of life.

At the Miami Physical Therapy Association

An article was written about her that was a winner in the Overcoming Adversity category of the America Inspired Contest. This contest celebrated extraordinary people making a difference across the United States.

Her transformation began in 2004 when her heartbroken father, who refused to believe his only daughter might never walk again, insisted she attend an event for SCI. That day changed Sabrina's life. Her motivation came from meeting with the stem cell advocate Bernard Siegel. He was a lawyer and the director of the Genetics Policy Institute.

Siegel said Sabrina's intellect and her ability to incorporate research into the program was impressive. "Sabrina has been a participant and speaker at seven annual World Stem Cell Summits," he said. "She is universally esteemed by researchers and fellow advocates. Through her inspiring presence, she lifts the world."

This was a great place for a presentation. There were many patients who came to hear us. We could see the staff cared, not just on the professional level, but on a personal level as well. I believe this is due to Clinical Director Miriam Marie Guanche, whose bright eyes and entrusting smile makes one feel comfortable and ready to offer support. She helped us with an unexpected donation to our challenge. I highly recommend that anyone in the Miami area with a SCI go to this place for your outpatient rehab. There is so much to be gained.

On Saturday morning, we made a trip to the Health & Fitness Expo, where we learned that our race numbers had been picked up by Team Achilles. The information booth gave us directions for the preferred parking for being a member of this group. We soon learned this was an organization that we needed to partner up with for other races. Not only did they pick up our race packets for us, there was a special parking area, tents to keep us out of the weather, and plenty of pre-race food. Then we had a special escort to the starting line and at the finish area there were more tents and post-race food. Wouldn't it be great if all races could be set up this way? Maybe more would come out for races.

Because Grant and Aaron were in a time zone three hours behind, when they wanted to get up at 3:00 a.m. and be on the road by 3:30 a.m. for a 6:00 a.m. start, I would have thought they would go to bed early. But at 11:00 p.m., they were still fine-tuning their racing chairs and then still working on packing the racing chairs into the van that evening. We arrived in the reserved starting area in what we thought was plenty of time, but found that there were so many athletes with disabilities competing that day that we had a hard time finding a parking spot. After unloading, we followed the rest of the athletes down the sidewalk toward lights and turned into the tent area. There were so many wheel-chairs, hand-cycles, amputees and visually-impaired runners with their guides, it was like our own city getting ready for this race. Volunteers were everywhere, asking if we needed anything. This is what the organization is all about.

Announcements were being made as to how soon the pre-race lineup would be, along with temperature readings to help guide us how to layer and hydrate. We were not prepared for the "buzz" and excitement that was building up for this marathon.

When the pre-race call to line up for the Team Achilles came, we had to have a vehicle escort us to the starting line through the crowds of regular runners. This also helped build the excitement for the crowd, which was already cheering with amazing yells of encouragement. We knew that they appreciated the challenges that each of us faced just to be there. And we hoped they, too, would build faith and courage to complete the challenge of the race they were about to undertake as well. We were soon on the street of the race where they had the buildings lit up in different colors for this special event. And a huge American flag was waving over the starting-line area.

What a glorious race this was going to be with such excitement and perfect weather.

At the Miami Marathon Starting Line

The cannon sounded and we were off, with a burst of motion. The last time I felt so exhilarated for the start of a race was 2010 in Ōita, Japan, which had more than 600 wheelers.

The only hills in this area were bridges, so we were always near water. As we breezed through the perfectly landscaped yards of expensive homes, we appreciated the smooth roads that allowed us the pleasure of just enjoying the push.

Because I am not a fast racer, the lead runners finally began to close the gap on me. The importance of this race necessitated a large flatbed truck to carry a multitude of reporters and TV crew who wanted the perfect shots of the sweating racers who were vying for the lead. Because this was such a flat course, my speed allowed me to push ahead at a faster pace. I was even able to hang with the pack of lead able-bodied racers. If anyone was watching the ESPN coverage closely, they may have caught a glimpse of my face.

I was beginning to fall behind the lead runners and was anticipating that I had only a few miles to the finish. Did I mention how nice an area we were in and that I was spending way too much time looking around like a tourist? A sudden burst of clapping and cheering jogged me out of my thoughts. It was the lead woman runner who was gaining ground on me. Then the finish line came into view and I began to turn on some more speed. They were getting the finish line ribbon into position. But when I saw the panic-stricken faces, I realized it was for the female winner to break and get that great shot of victory for the cameras. I realized that if I kept up the speed, I would be the one who ruined her photo! Not to mention the dismay of the reporters and the ESPN crew. So, I pulled off to the side, as generally it is the runners who have the right of way. Once the winner's moment was captured, I began to head to the finish line myself. Again, the crowd erupted with applause, but this time it was for me. A couple of the race officials came up to shake my hand, thanking me for preserving their photographic moment. Actually, I felt inspired by her achievement. You see, the wheelchair racers had started 10 minutes ahead of the runners. This meant that she had covered that same race about half a minute per mile faster than I did. I believe she was the same woman that I saw when she won the 2008 Ironman World Championship in my area of Louisville, Kentucky.

This race will go onto my list of repeats. However, I want to have a really good rest beforehand instead of racing in three other marathons in three weeks. I will also push it throughout and leave the sightseeing until later. I vowed to enjoy a few extra days instead of rushing back to work.

———

RACE RESULTS

Seven Wheelchair Racers participated in the race,
with around 30 hand-cyclists.

4th (02:08:24) – Grant Berthiaume

6th (02:28:55) – Aaron Roux

7th (02:35:05) – Paul Erway

———

Behind the Scenes

During our speaking presentation, one gentleman asked some great questions. We were told that he was the founder/owner of Miami Physical Therapy Associates, Inc. After our talk, he asked if we had heard of Shake-A-Leg?

"No, I really can't shake my leg," I laughed. "Or even move it!"

He told us that it was a program just a half-mile down the street on the bay that led to the ocean where they had adaptive sailing and kayaking.

"I am good friends with the director there and want to take you down to see their program," he said.

This was Friday afternoon. Our only plans were to pick up the race packets on Saturday and then do the race early Sunday and fly home that afternoon.

So we loaded up and followed him to an area that opens to a fantastic view of yachts and sailboats on beautiful blue water. On this a warm, sunny day, how could anything be such an adventure?

We were introduced to Harry Horgan, CEO, who told us the history of his program and how they are putting together a grant request to the Christopher & Dana Reeve Foundation for another sailboat. Our challenge might help in ways we had not expected. He had someone from his organization give us a tour of the facility. We saw so many people there with different disabilities who were either finishing, chatting at tables, or getting ready for their turn on the water.

We headed down one of the docks, where an individual was lying flat in this sailboat that was coming in. A volunteer was on the dock to guide the boat as it got close enough to tie up. The volunteer then helped the gentleman out of the boat. To our astonishment, the man had no arms and had been sailing his vessel on his own with only his feet! How many places would someone get this opportunity?

Enjoying the Miami sun

We went to the next dock where there were a lot of wheelchairs sitting empty. The people that used them were sailing in the bay or ocean. The director said the volunteers were medical students who were there to experience what people with disabilities have to go through in life, as well as see what they can enjoy if they embrace their disability and not let it hold them back.

Harry asked us to stick around and give a small talk to this set of volunteers about our challenge. We started to wrap up when Harry came out to say goodbye. Then he asked us, "What are you doing tomorrow? Do you want to try this and go out sailing yourselves?"

I live in Kentucky so I don't get to see such splendor nor experience all the sensuousness that the ocean has to offer, to say nothing of having this type of weather in January. We wanted to jump for joy. With a resounding "Yes!" from all three of us, it was set for noon the following day.

When you get experiences like these, who would dare to not take on challenges that can lead to great enjoyment along the way?

———

Possibilities

"Life is a journey, not a destination."

— Ralph Waldo Emerson —

MARATHON #5
Myrtle Beach, South Carolina

"Guidance"

———

February 16, 2013
7:00 a.m.

By this time, we had come in contact with people, such as Mark Zenobia, who had been a tremendous asset for us. When there was little money to get us to a race, he personally made a donation. He provided transportation and meals to support us in this race. He has been a light of GUIDANCE for us through this whole challenge.

This shows the dedication of participants: "Thank you to our participants for showing the world that the Myrtle Beach Marathon attracts a wild group of passionate runners!" – taken from the race website. For a few days every February, the streets of Myrtle Beach are transformed into a jungle scene that provides the backdrop to an unforgettable experience. The proceeds go to Rare Species Fund. As one might expect, they had all kinds of wild animals on display, including baby tigers and chimpanzees. Some race winners even had their pictures taken with the animals.

Though not the largest, the expo was very unique. At Pelican's Ballpark, there were trained dogs carrying a basket around to each person to ask for money. Once furnished, the dogs would take it back to a central point. Should you choose not to donate, the pooches would shadow you until you did what was expected. Grant and Aaron had told a few people about our challenge. And before long, word spread. When it came time for the start of the race, the announcer explained why we were there and gave out the information to our website.

At the Myrtle Beach Marathon Starting Line

This was the first weekend of doing a marathon in one state on Saturday, then traveling by whatever means necessary to another state to battle the next marathon. Two marathons in 24 hours. Thus, I was not at this race because I was traveling ahead to Birmingham, Alabama. This provided a safety net should anything happen if my teammates could not make the trip. This way, as a team, we could still get all 50 marathons completed. I was also tasked with getting us registered with race numbers in hand when they arrived at this next event. So, I shall do this event in Myrtle Beach another year.

The hotel in Myrtle Beach was three miles from where the race began. This was the first race in which any of us had to use this as a warm-up for the marathon. Grant and Aaron got to the start in plenty of time, ready and raring to go. As they are waiting for the start signal, a pungent smell drifted in. It was coming, they realized, from Bubbles the elephant, a mere 15 feet from the starting line. Grant and Aaron thought it was neat when they cued Bubbles to give her elephant trumpet call as part of getting ready to start the race.

The race was very scenic, running close to the shoreline. You can't beat the salty scent, sounds of the waves, the appearance of diamonds sparkling in them with seagulls flying so effortlessly overhead.

Grant took the lead and found that the course was not well-marked, causing him to get off course for two blocks before realizing he needed to turn back toward the ocean. He found his way back on course and then directed Aaron.

Racing at sea level is nice because you don't need to worry about altitude. Moreover, the course had no hills; the elevation chart showed 56 feet as the highest point. More than that, a big plus was the smooth roads. The difficult part was coming into the finish and realizing they still had to do another three miles back to the hotel to get into their everyday chairs. A total of 32 miles that day.

RACE RESULTS

7,000 runners, 3 Hand-Crank Wheelchairs and 2 Racing Wheelchairs

1st (02:08:32) – Grant Berthiaume

2nd (02:25:48) – Aaron Roux

Behind the Scenes

The Christopher & Dana Reeve Foundation has some outstanding supporters associated with their organization. We met one member at this race. Mark Zenobia not only drove two hours to meet Grant and Aaron, but they also accepted his dinner invitation. Mark stayed at a hotel so he could get up early to be there for the start of the race. He also took all kinds of photos and made sure Grant and Aaron got back safely.

Grant at the Finish Line

As we progressed through this challenge, Mark was there to help guide us, help with contacts at some of the locations, and on many times went to bat for us with things that come up with CDRF. There was even a stretch when there was little money for us to make it to a race, so he made a donation that helped carry us through. He was a guiding light for us through this whole challenge and we were blessed to have his support. Not just for us, but for all persons with spinal cord injuries in the United States. He even helped with guidance and direction for the writing of this book.

———

Possibilities

"If you are not willing to risk the unusual, you will have to settle for the ordinary."

- Jim Rohn -

MARATHON #6
Birmingham, Alabama

"Overcoming Fear"

February 17, 2013
8:00 a.m.

Unique to this weekend was a new twist to our challenge. We termed it our back-to-back marathons. This means having the Saturday race in Myrtle Beach and then hurrying off to drive the 510 miles to Birmingham to race the next day.

But suddenly there was a frantic message from Grant, who informed us that we may not be able to participate in the marathon. He called me in the middle of a work day, which was a first, then described the situation. (Note: I do not like problems for they are so negative. A "situation" is more positive, for there may be a way to work through things.)

According to the fine print on the race website, it stated that wheelchair athletes would be limited to only the half marathon. Panic! We had set out to do full marathons. This could totally derail our goal to complete the 50 full marathons challenge. After discussing the matter, Grant sent a carefully worded email to the race director to see if she could make an exception to the rules. We pleaded our case, told her of our challenge goal and how we were prepared for the 26.2 miles in hopes of somehow getting her to change her mind. After all, we were unique and not just out to just do a single race.

Fortunately, we knew of a great wheelchair team based in Birmingham, the Lakeshore Foundation. We contacted Mandy Goff, the Associate Director of Athletics, who also is the USA Wheelchair Rugby program manager. She knew of Aaron, because rugby is his second sport. Mandy's friend Susan Katz, a Paralympian, was coming to town with the intention of competing in the full marathon using her racing wheelchair. She told us that she would definitely be looking into this situation.

Finally, three days later, we found our fear was unwarranted when the Race Director, Jill Edwards, responded that the information on the website was incorrect.

"That was a mistake on our website and if you go back now you will see that the sentence has been taken off," Jill said. "The full marathon is open to wheelchair athletes." Whew!

We also got an email from Mandy that her friend, Susan Katz, received a personal phone call from Jill Edwards stating that the info on the website had not been taken off from the previous year and that she was wanting more racing wheelchairs in her event and she was now working on getting bike guides for our division as well. Susan also said that Jill was very nice and was upset to think that we would not be allowed in the full marathon.

First there was the scare that we may not be able to race in this marathon, which would affect our schedule, flight plans ... the list could go on and on. Wheelchair races would be limited to half marathons, which causes panic to strike because we set out to do full marathons. However, with fine-tuning our efforts and OVERCOMING FEAR, we faced the obstacles and were successful.

Once again, situations are positive. They are things that can be worked out. And we were back on our schedule.

Now it was time to work on the daunting task of how to get logistically from the finish line of one marathon in Myrtle Beach, South Carolina, to the starting line of the marathon in Birmingham, Alabama, the following morning. This included managing to get the race packets from the race expo that closed at 6:00 p.m., with no race-day pick-up, and get a little rest before another early cold morning 26.2-mile race.

This is Chris, a.k.a. "Wonder Woman." She flew into town for the marathon. Her Invisible Jet was double parked outside.

Our plans for the 50-marathon challenge began in the fall of 2010. To our dismay, some of the dates for the races had changed by 2013, either moved ahead or back by several weeks in the calendar. For someone planning on one or two of these races in a year, that would not be a big deal. But we had a race every weekend. Not to mention that in some races wheelchair athletes were only going to be allowed to enter the half marathon or be totally excluded from the race.

There was also the potential for issues with equipment, such as broken
parts, flat tires, as well as the same aches and pains as a runner. Thus,
we decided to race as a team. Considering the Myrtle Beach and
Birmingham races were the first back-to-back experience, it was
determined that I would skip the Saturday event and go directly to
Birmingham. This plan allowed me to arrive in time to gather the race
packets before the health expo closed, secure our hotel accommoda-
tions, and purchase our race supplies, such as fluids and supplements.
Once Aaron and Grant arrived in Birmingham, I was able to pick them
up after they had turned in the rental vehicle and get us all settled
into the hotel.

Once again, luck would be on our side as we found a hotel in
Birmingham just on the other side of Linn Park where the race would
begin and end. This allowed us to change from our everyday chairs to
our racing chairs in the warmth of the hotel lobby and return without
worries, for this was going to be a cold one.

At the Birmingham Marathon Starting Line

We feel it is important that we should share this inspiring story
in the history of this race with this excerpt from the website:
"A Marathon for Love":

---

*"It's really a love story. The Mercedes Marathon, a test of endurance and
determination, a goal that drives ordinary people to train for months, is
really just a love story. It's a love story between a boy named Matt and his
daddy named Paul.*

*Matt was born with Down syndrome 17 years ago. But not only did he
have Down syndrome, he also had the heart defect that often accompanies
the diagnosis. A sick little boy, Matt required open-heart surgery, and the
whole idea frightened his parents, Paul and Cinna Sotherland.*

*Cinna vividly remembers being at UAB hospital with Matt and Paul just
before Matt was to have his open-heart surgery. The family was standing
at one of the big windows at the end of the hallway that looked out over
the streets of downtown. Runners, competing in the old Vulcan Marathon,
were racing by, and Paul — who ran a little, just for exercise — looked
down at his tiny son and made one promise. 'You pull through this, Matt,
and next year, Daddy will run a marathon for you,' Paul pledged.*

*Tough little Matt kept his end of the bargain, and Daddy began training.
Together they tackled the challenges ahead: Matt's challenges that come as
a part of the Down syndrome diagnosis, and Paul's determination to run
26.2 miles in honor of the son he so loves. During his training, Paul looked
for guidance and motivation, and even good running shoes, from Valerie
McLean, the owner of The Trak Shak running shops. Paul did run the
Vulcan Marathon the next year, and then kept on running, completing 19
marathons and half marathons too numerous to count. But it was really
Valerie who took the inspiration from Paul and Matt.*

She helped organize a half-marathon to benefit The Early Intervention

Program (now The Bell Center), the place where Cinna and Paul brought Matt to receive critical therapies, and over the next five years, the Freeze Your Half Off Half-Marathon grew into a first-class event. Valerie knew it was time to take the event to a greater level, and in 2002 transformed the Freeze Your Half Off into the Mercedes Marathon and Half Marathon. Proceeds from the event are given annually to The Bell Center for Early Intervention Programs."

But, from our perspective, it was evident that they really do need to go back and change the name to the original Freeze Your Half Off, for it was rather cold the entire day.

We were pleasantly surprised to find that Jill Edwards was there. She had not only provided us with the bike guides, but had arranged prize money also. This was the first monetary reward for our challenge. Another surprise was our finishing times. Grant, despite doing back-to-back marathons with a very long drive in between, placed first with a time of 2:13:19. Aaron had a little more trouble, finishing third with a time of 2:54:17. I was upbeat that I only lagged behind by 10 minutes. Aaron was shocked that Susan Katz had beaten me by a full two and half minutes. My response was that she is a Paralympian! To which Aaron's reply was, "Yeah, but that is in wheelchair basketball, not racing!"

Our weekend continued into Monday with a presentation at HealthSouth Rehabilitation Hospital. Jinnie Lacey, the Rehabilitation Liaison, was pleased that we would want to take an extra day to speak to the therapists and patients. Grant and Aaron were feeling sluggish that morning, probably due to two marathons in as many days. They worried that the audience would not be interested in listening to three ordinary guys. On the same campus was housed the Paralympic athletes in training. Jinnie had arranged a TV station to interview us, so I told them, "Game time, guys. They're going to love us!"

We were amazed when we saw how many therapists, patients, and staff members came to hear us in the therapy gym. There were a few questions while the television cameras filmed us. Based on the questions at the end, we knew they were engaged and listening. We later found out that the staff had never seen any of the Paralympic athletes from the other facility unless one of them sustained an injury. They really wanted to hear us and learn how we got started. And seeing a racing wheelchair up close seemed to be new to them. This reassured us that we needed to take the time to tell as many as we could about this challenge. Our hope was that we may help one of their patients if we can relay our story.

RACE RESULTS

Male Wheelchair

1st (02:13:19) – Grant Berthiaume

2nd (02:54:17) – Aaron Roux

4th (03:04:40) – Paul Erway

Female Wheelchair

3rd (03:02:03) – Susan Katz

Behind the Scenes

Our presentation at the rehab facility was what helped to convey what we were trying to do with this challenge. There was one member of the audience who had endless questions throughout the entire presentation. After we had finished, she came up to us and introduced herself as the Medical Director of this HealthSouth facility. She was concerned to know about how we were doing this financially. We explained that we were on a constant mission to find sponsorships, large or small. We felt that some potential contacts would fear for our failure and would not sponsor us when they found out that this would be the first time a wheelchair athlete would attempt doing 50 marathons in one year, let alone in all 50 states. Up until now, we had been paying for everything ourselves on a leap of faith. We fervently hoped that our efforts would trigger enough publicity that someone would want to sponsor us, rather than the plethora of ones that say, "We can give you a T-shirt." We get a T-shirt every race we enter.

The best thing about meeting this doctor was that she was headed to a national meeting with all the other HealthSouth locations throughout the United States. I knew there were numerous locations since there are some locations even in my marketing area for Superior Van & Mobility. I called on four of their locations. She informed us that this was a great challenge, but even better for a great cause and she would do her best to ask the right people to help us complete this challenge with a good sponsorship.

I have seen their gracious sponsorship levels as with my friend Doug Hair, a quad who has won gold medals at the Paralympic Games, an accomplished lawyer who even consulted Christopher Reeve when he had his accident. Also, Mark Wellman, the extreme athlete who, after a climbing accident left him paralyzed from the waist down, had come back to climb Yosemite National Park's Half Dome and El Capitan. This could be a great fit because we could easily arrange to speak at all of their locations and touch more lives than we had ever hoped for.

Possibilities

"Being challenged in life is inevitable, being defeated is optional."

— Roger Crawford —

MARATHON #7
New Orleans, Louisiana

"Gratitude"

_____

February 24, 2013
7:00 a.m.

Laissez Les Bons Temps Rouler (Lay-say lay bawn tawn roulay – lay-zay le bohn tohn roo-lay) – The New Orleans motto in French for "Let the good times roll."

And boy did we roll. This race was among our top favorite races because of the team of organizers Rock 'n' Roll Marathon and our friend Jennifer Nanista, who heads up the racing wheelchair division. It was also exhilarating to have two rehab facilities requesting our presence — one in Baton Rouge and the other in New Orleans.

This trip was sponsored by Superior Van & Mobility to help defray some of the costs. As a sign of our GRATITUDE, we called on each of the Superior locations in the region. At the New Orleans dealership, we had the opportunity to meet a delightful customer who showed her indebtedness for her accessible vehicle and the service she had received. She gave back by being a mentor for the local rehabilitation center.

Superior Van & Mobility is able to adapt vehicles for a person with a disability. At this writing, there are nine dealerships in four states and they were willing to sponsor us in those four states. Because I am employed by this company, I was still working full-time during the year while doing our race events. The good thing about representing this company is that they were chosen as the number-one company in the United States by BraunAbility, a leader in manufacturing wheelchair accessible vans and lifts. Part of the criteria is customer service; we know anyone we recommend to Superior Van & Mobility will receive great customer service.

Our first scheduled stop took us to Baton Rouge Rehab Hospital where we met Roxane Bingham. She was the rehabilitation liaison who was very knowledgeable and remarkably supportive to wheelchair sports. She fits her position perfectly with her energy and friendliness.

With Courtney Laser and Roxane Bingham
from the Baton Rouge Rehabilitation Hospital

Roxane gave us a tour of the rehab and we briefly met with staff members as they came by, along with other key people. They would later join us for lunch after the talk. The number of people who came in to hear us was astounding. There was a mix of past patients, current patients, as well as therapists and staff. Even the coach of the wheelchair tennis team came. With so many present, we wondered if there was anyone else in the other areas of the facility. Roxane Bingham has my sincere gratitude for her service in helping in so many ways for people with disabilities in this community. Her caring goes well beyond her normal paid work week. In fact, she makes it her life mission to help others even if it involves long days and weekends. She is a blessing.

On the return trip to New Orleans, we encountered one of the longest bridges we had ever seen: the Lake Pontchartrain Causeway Bridge. It passed over the open ocean and swamp land. We learned we were near the site of the filming of one of the reality shows. Because it was filmed in a swampy area, we all had thoughts of alligators being an issue. For that matter, the crews involved in the construction of this 23.83 miles of bridge supported by more than 9,000 concrete pilings probably had to keep their wits about them for constantly looking out for the gators. I was so glad to only be doing the road race in the city.

*The guys meet another colorful character named David Deneire
at the Rock 'n' Roll Mardi Gras Expo*

Our next stop the following day brought us to the Touro Rehabilitation Center, where we were going to get a taste of how flat of a race this would be.

Touro Rehabilitation Center is a regional referral center and home to a nationally recognized program for brain and spinal cord injury, as well as comprehensive inpatient rehabilitation. In 1929, Touro was one of the first hospitals in the United States to have a physical therapy department. Today, TRC remains proud of its history of excellence in rehabilitation.

At the New Orleans Marathon Finish Line

It might be in the old part of town in an older building, but it is the people who make a difference and the staff made it seem new and exciting. They were eager to hear what we had to say about our challenge. Rehab Services Educator Maureen Herring was a big help with directions and arranging with the marketing department to get the word out to the media.

The race in New Orleans is one of the Rock 'n' Roll Series of marathons. We were glad to have the assistance of one of our friends, Jennifer Nanista from the organization, as this race is termed a point-to-point event. This requires someone to get our everyday chairs from the starting area to the finish area, once we transfer into our racing chairs. And thanks to Jennifer, this all happened according to plan.

Have I told you yet how flat this race will be? The elevation chart shows the start of the race at five feet above sea level, dropping to two feet below in general areas, raising to 15 feet then below sea level in others. This is the kind of race Aaron loves, for he is not the best hill climber, thus it is right up his alley. We loved having the live jazz bands and the local community cheering us on. Despite all the destruction resulting from Hurricane Katrina years ago, the city had come together and it looked great. The Super Bowl had been played there just a couple of weeks before. Then there was the famous Mardi Gras. And now this race. No wonder the waiters and waitresses looked tired. There had been a lot of partying going on before the athletes came into town.

RACE RESULTS

1st (02:14:51) – Grant Berthiaume

2nd (02:52:39) – Aaron Roux

3rd (02:59:20) – Paul Erway

Behind the Scenes

Superior Van & Mobility was our sponsor to help defray some of the costs in this event and we went to each of the company's locations. The first was in Baton Rouge where we had our picture taken with the staff and I got some work done while there. The following day we were at the New Orleans dealership. We met one of their delightful customers, Usha Sadhwani. She raved about the service she got at Superior and will always be getting her new wheelchair-accessible vans from them because of that. As a member of Touro Rehabilitation Center SCI Support Group, she heard we were coming to speak, but could not attend. She asked us to join her and her friends downtown in the French Quarter for dinner at Superior Seafood. (Yes, I like the name too.) We enjoyed some of the local cuisine for which New Orleans is famous and I really filled up on fresh seafood while I had the chance because I live so far inland. The other local food favorite that all tourists have to partake in are beignets — square, French-style doughnuts at Café du Monde.

The experience was a joy. While we were downtown, we got a little time to wheel around that area and see some of the sites that one may see in the pictures in magazines or from their friends' trips. Still hanging on the limbs of trees were the necklaces that are thrown from Mardi Gras floats or broken ones lying in the streets that were missed by the cleanup sweeper. To think what devastation it must have been with Hurricane Katrina through her mighty gales upon the waters to bring so much to cover these buildings, and yet here they still stand with so much history that they have seen and experienced.

———

Possibilities

"Make a gift of your life and lift all mankind by being kind, considerate, forgiving, and compassionate at all times, in all places, and under all conditions, with everyone as well as yourself. This is the greatest gift anyone can give."

— David Hawkins —

MARATHON #8
Albany, Georgia

"Sweetness"

—

March 2, 2013
8:00 a.m.

We knew we were in for a treat when signing up for this race.

Commercials for the Snickers candy bar promote, "You're just not yourself until you have a Snickers." We discovered the importance of SWEETNESS after Snickers, the main race sponsor, produced a treat called the "Marathon Bar." Located in the town of Albany is the factory that roasts all the peanuts used in all of the Snickers products. Employees from the factory were handing out the bars at the race health expo. They had given up their personal time to come and hand out a product that they personally had a hand in making. They were able to see how their products make people smile, and to know they have a part in making people stay fit by powering them in the sport of running.

The schedule of 50 marathons in 50 states takes some time in organizing, so thank you to Grant, who got it all started two and half years before the challenge began. Since that winter of 2010, marathons changed their week or month from the previous year or there were even ones that did not repeat. We had to find new ones that would fit into our schedule so we could accomplish our challenge. The race in Albany happened to be in one of those states that would not fit in the big-city race and was not included in the Rock 'n' Roll Series. This required traveling a little farther out, which put us away from any airport — or even a rehab facility in the area where we could have given a presentation.

At the Starting Line of the Snickers Marathon in Albany

Regarding the marathons, we prefer to race in a straight line for a long distance because the fewer turns we have to take, the better and faster. Every time we reach up to steer through the tight turns, our momentum slows, making it harder to get back up to speed. But we knew we might end up with a slower pace for this one because we had 49 turns in the 26.2 miles. Even if it's a slight turn in which we can "hip" the chair and not interrupt forward pushing, we still do not get a full, good, hard push. There were bound to be quite a few hippings going on, such as where the race package describes "travel around Lake Loretta."

The race involved more than 50 separate turns throughout the route. In the beginning alone, we took two rights, a left, a right, a left, a right, a left, a right, two lefts … you get the picture.

You see, in wheelchair racing it is less energy spent and faster to have straight road races, so this one turned out to be bitter-SWEETNESS as far as the course goes.

RACE RESULTS

600 runners; 6 wheelers

1st (02:07:03) – Grant Berthiaume

2nd (02:16:10) – Aaron Roux

3rd (03:05:20) – Paul Erway

Behind the Scenes

I drove down from Kentucky rather then fly so we'd have access to a vehicle in which all three of us could fit. Remember, we still did not have a major sponsor and were trying to save where we could. I was at the Atlanta airport when Grant and Aaron arrived, and drove the two hours to Albany in time to make the fitness expo on Friday night.

We shared a room at the hotel. And when there are three guys, as guys go, we do not share the same bed, which means there also has to be a roll-away bed or someone sleeps on the floor. We have three everyday chairs and when we fly with our racing chairs there are things we have to do to get them past security. This means that most evenings, our time is spent preparing our racing chair for the next event.

(Remember the comment from the Houston, Texas, race that we carry spare tires and CO2 cartridges so we do not ruin the expensive disc wheels? Well, airport security does not like to have them on our chair, so the cartridges have to be put in a checked bag or we hide them in our seat cushions in the hope of not being caught. I always have a checked bag, but Grant takes his chances because he does not like baggage claim and packs very light. We always check our racing wheelchairs at the gate at the same time the airline checks our everyday chairs so we can see that when it is brought back to us it is OK. If we let them put it through as a bag, nobody knows who is to blame if there's a problem. There's nothing worse than finding, when you get to your destination, that you can't race because some suitcase shifted during the flight and destroyed your chair.)

We then lubricate the wheel bearings because maybe it was raining during the last race or it was dusty. You certainly want your chair to roll as easily as possible. Then we inspect and air the tires, because we don't want any flats. I run about 210 psi, where Grant is about 180 because he is much lighter. To do this, we have to take our own air pump, which is another security issue and it's heavy. We check our racing gloves and liners and apply the Spider Tack, which helps us grip our push-rims. Next, we get our water container ready to attach because our gloves Velcro our hands closed and we cannot grasp a cup of water at the aid stations in a race; carrying our own hydration is crucial.

As you can see, we don't just show up to a race, put our sneakers on and stretch a little before the start. It takes us a good amount of time to prepare for each event.

So I picked the others up late Friday afternoon, we drove to the expo, then the hotel, prepared the chairs, finished the race in a timely fashion, got back to the hotel, and prepared the chairs to fly on a plane again. At this point, we were in a hurry mode because this was another back-to-back weekend and we needed to get back to Atlanta for a flight to Little Rock, Arkansas. Luckily, the friend we mentioned who we met at the very first marathon picked up our race packets because by the time we landed it would have been too late; the fitness expo was already closed.

We prepared the chairs again for an early start for the next marathon, finished again in a timely manner to then catch a flight back to Atlanta, to get there in time for the flight back to Arizona. Is there anybody tired yet from this weekend and what extra we had to go through? Why couldn't we just fly from Little Rock? No sponsorship money to buy tickets with extra stops. You would think there would be less flight, less jet fuel used, but, no, we had this extra flying on top of making everything easy for the airlines to inspect our two chairs each, air pump, and luggage.

Possibilities

"The future is not a gift – it is an achievement."

— Harry Lauder —

"Few people take objectives really seriously. They put average effort into too many things, rather than superior thought and effort into a few important things. People who achieve the most are selective as well as determined."

— Richard Hoch —

MARATHON #9
Little Rock, Arkansas

"Goal-Setting"

———

March 3, 2013
7:00 a.m.

This was a tough race for Aaron and Grant. It was not quite as bad as the very first in Jackson, Mississippi, but was another event that added to our challenge, philosophy, and GOAL-SETTING in that we did not go out to find the easiest races in each state. Whatever comes, we were prepared to take on the challenge: even hill after hill, we strove for the end, even with back-to-back marathons with little sleep.

This marathon included some pleasant things that help make doing these races so much fun, even with the challenges that we endured to get there, race and get home, and get ready for work the next day.

Challenge: Aaron was late booking the flight. He had to fly out three hours after Grant from Atlanta, where I had dropped them off. This allowed Grant to pick up the rental as soon as he landed and traverse right to the expo to pick up race numbers just before registration was to close. Aaron had failed to register, but fortunately the director had heard of our 50-marathons challenge and did not charge Aaron an entry fee. Grant suspected it was timely to get them out of there because they were ready to close up the health expo. But this was helpful to us as we still were struggling with sponsorship money. That was one of the reasons I had to miss this one, but the other benefit was it also worked the best for logistics.

Grant went back to the hotel that was near the airport and checked in. He went to grab his dinner and, lo and behold, there was Becky, the Half Marathon Maniac who we met the very first race. Her friend Linda was with her for this race so Grant enjoyed the company of friends while dining. Becky and Linda always wear different outfits for every race and this might have been their best one of the year. The theme of this race is "The Wild West," so those two were decked out. They were so authentic they looked like they came from an old postcard — right down to six shooters in their holsters, ready to draw.

After dinner, it was time for Grant to go back to the airport and pick up Aaron. They needed to get the chairs ready for another early morning start. They would only have two to three hours of rest, as they had just completed a marathon on Saturday, just one day earlier.

This race had five racing wheelchairs and one hand-cyclist at the starting line. The oddest thing happened: as the race director started the count-down from 10, the hand-cyclists took off immediately. The other racing chairs were looking at each other and turning around to the runners as if to say, "What is going on?" Sure enough, when the gun sounded only the racing chairs took off – the hand-cyclists had a 30-foot jump! But no worries, they found out they all ended up beating the hand-cyclists' time by more than an hour, with Grant being twice as fast.

This was a tough race — not as bad as the first, but hard. We did not go out to find the easiest races in each state, but only the ones that could fit into our schedule. Grant described this race as going up a tough hill right off, then going a while on the flat stretch, but then up another hill to another flat area, then back up another hill. He never remembered any downhills, maybe this was due to the back-to-back marathons they did with little sleep in between and exhaustion was setting in. Grant was sure the website showed downhills, but he couldn't remember any.

The benefit, though, was the finish line. We would have to say this was, in our opinion, the top one for all the races that we were doing for the year. True to the theme of "The Wild West," there was not only country line and swing dancing with lots of barbecue, but a huge spread of breakfast food as well.

Grant at the Little Rock Finish Line

The finish medal (given to each one who finished the race): "gaudy," according to Grant, "As big as a dinner plate." This is impressive to have one but if you have another flight, packing this with your racing chair and luggage for a two-race weekend was a challenge in itself. We continually reminded ourselves that if this was an easy challenge that everyone would be doing it and we would not be the first wheelchairs to do a marathon in every state. But difficulty did not deter us. When we did our GOAL-SETTING at the beginning of the challenge, we decided we wanted to raise awareness for the Christopher & Dana Reeve Foundation; this is truly what kept us going through all the tough times.

_____

RACE RESULTS

1st (02:16:26) – Grant Berthiaume

2nd (03:02:37) – Aaron

Had I been there I would NOT have been the oldest wheelchair racer. Richard Vaughn, at age 60, did it in 4:58:12

_____

Behind the Scenes

Car rental companies try their best to adhere to the Americans with Disabilities Act (ADA), which is a set of rules and regulations to make services accessible for a person with a disability … as much as possible. The companies are supposed to provide hand controls on vehicles if a person with a disability needs to rent the car to drive, but they do require 48-hour notice. This gives them the two to three hours required to install the hand controls. This would prove to be the first of many hindrances for us in the coming year of travels. Grant used a lower-priced, lesser-known company to rent the vehicle this time and found that a bargain-basement deal was also in the controls they use.

Portable hand controls may work a little differently than the regular bolted-on mechanical hand controls. But they can be attached to the gas and brake pedals directly with Velcro or wing nuts to plates in a matter of minutes. Most athletes have a set, so if our own vehicle breaks down we can make use of a friend's car, as well as being able to take a vehicle for a test drive. The rental companies frown on us installing our own due to their insurance regulations.

In his hurry to leave the airport to get to the expo in time, Grant failed to check the installation of the portable hand controls. Within 10 minutes of getting on the road, the controls fell off the gas pedal. Rental companies need to realize we could avoid an accident by using our own and we definitely make sure they are installed because we don't like to have accidents ourselves.

––––––

Possibilities

"It's determination and commitment to an unrelenting pursuit of your goal that will enable you to attain the success you seek."
— Mario Andretti —

"The victory of success is half won when one gains the habit of setting goals and achieving them. Even the most tedious chore will become endurable as you parade through each day convinced that every task, no matter how menial or boring, brings you closer to fulfilling your dreams."
— Og Mandino —

MARATHON #10
Los Angeles, California

"Flexible"

———

March 17, 2013
7:00 a.m.

There were so many reasons why we were looking forward to this race. For me, the most outstanding thing would be the weather — just the pleasure to be in the warm sun again. It seemed that Old Man Winter had come with a vengeance for 2013 in the Northeast and that included my area of Kentucky. It was also much easier to get about with not having to wear all the extra clothing or worry about slippery surfaces to wheel on.

Our search to find a rehab facility that would want us to deliver our message revealed a unique connection for our cause. There is, of course, the Casa Colina Center for Rehabilitation, and Rancho Los Amigos National Rehabilitation Center in California. However, I discovered that the Next Step Fitness Center had ties with Frazier Rehab in Louisville. The president of Next Step is Janne Kouri, who is 6 feet, 4 inches tall and weighs 290 pounds. Janne was an outstanding college football player. His life restarted on a spring day while on the beach playing volleyball, when in between sets he went to cool off with a dip into the ocean. Unfortunately, he dove into a sand bar and broke his neck.

His supportive family rallied behind him, and made it their mission
to seek the best help available. They refused to believe his doctor, who
told them that Janne would never walk again. In their relentless search,
they found Dr. Susan Harkema whose practice is at Frazier Rehab in
Louisville, Kentucky. The rehab program that Janne's family wanted him
to be involved with was the very same that Dr. Harkema had developed
at Frazier Rehab when she was caring for Christopher Reeve.

After spending a year in Kentucky, Janne returned home to California
unable to find the same type of program to keep him going. He took the
initiative to start his own with the goal that he would also be helping
others. This is exactly what we wanted to be a part of, so I contacted
Janne. I learned later that Janne and I had met at Frazier Rehab, where
I was instrumental in helping him get a rental wheelchair-accessible
van from Superior Van & Mobility while they were working
with Dr. Harkema.

Our speaking arrangements at Next Step Fitness of California were made
well in advance of our arrival in Los Angeles. Wouldn't you know, the day
before, the organizers of the LA Marathon scheduled a press conference
at the Fitness Expo the exact same day and time as our appointment!
This is why we have learned how to be FLEXIBLE because "the show
must go on," so we used the "divide and conquer" strategy to achieve
our goal. Grant does not like to speak before a large crowd or even a few
people, so he chose to go to the Fitness Expo where Janne would do most
of the talking. That left Aaron and me to give our full presentation to all
of the patients and staff at Next Step Fitness.

This worked well for Aaron and me, but not for Grant and Janne or
the other top wheelchair athletes who were ready to share their story.
They waited for over an hour and still no TV press or newspaper
reporters showed.

Aaron and I did not have any TV crew at our presentation either, but it was still fun and relaxing with pizza brought for everyone to enjoy. We were sure to thank the therapists for how much we appreciated their efforts in everything they are doing.

(Should anyone want to see how much Janne has improved, just Google his name along with Good Morning America and see him dance with his wife.)

Visiting with Next Step Fitness in Lawndale, California

There was a lot of support at this race by Jairo and Laura Rivera who tried to request the race sponsor to cover our entry fee; happily, they did. They even picked us up at the airport and transported us to Next Step Fitness, which was not related to their race at all. A large tent was erected at Dodgers Stadium to provide a warm-up area for the wheelchair racers and hand-cyclists. It was also supplied with drinks and snacks; plus, helpful volunteers were such an asset. This type of reinforcement was again provided at the finish line. These things made this one of the top races for the wheelchair division races, a must to put on your bucket list before you stop racing.

Grant had raced this one before and had warned us of a steep and very long hill that was pretty brutal. However, the highlight of this year was a middle school drum unit that positioned themselves alongside this killer hill and used their big Chinese war drums to boom as encouragement to us up this major obstacle. Their enthusiasm sure did help us. We could not imagine that they had that much energy for the rest of the racers, who were coming behind us. It testifies to how tough that hill was because I was able to get so far out in front of Aaron that he could not make up the time. This may be one of those few occasions that my time was going to be better than Aaron's, because he is not a hill climber.

The best part, as Grant told us, was the end.

Grant with the Achilles Girls after the LA Marathon

"Once you make it through the first 20 miles, the rest is going to be easy," he said. He was not kidding. It seemed that after I reached the top, I was coasting quite a bit. The ocean views were stupendous. Such a warm and sunny day in February with the ocean breeze, sound of seagulls and the graceful palm trees. A pretty wonderful treat for a guy from Kentucky. All this made this trip worth all the effort.

———

RACE RESULTS

23,001 Total Participants, which consisted of 37 wheelchair racers (9 Women and 28 Men) and 49 hand-cycles. This was a great turnout for athletes with a disability.

11th (01:54:46) - Grant Berthiaume

20th (02:45:20) - Paul Erway

21st (02:48:46) - Aaron Roux

———

Behind The Scenes

We had a nice surprise when we arrived at the Los Angeles Convention Center, as there seemed to be quite a few people using wheelchairs rolling around. "The race really can't have that many wheelchairs or hand-cyclist entries in it, can it?" we wondered. We learned that there are six of these Ability Expos positioned around the United States and the one in California happened to be going on at the same time in the same convention center as the Marathon Fitness Expo. Once we picked up our race packets with our bid numbers for the race, we took time to visit all the exhibits in the Ability Expo.

There were more than 100 exhibit booths, two workshop areas and even an events arena for demonstrations like wheelchair basketball, quad rugby, and other exciting programs that needed a large area to demonstrate. The first thing we saw when entering the Ability Expo was the BraunAbility display and, nicknamed "Mr. Entervan," the employee who specializes in the product that BraunAbility manufactures and which Superior Van & Mobility (SVM) distributes throughout a four-state area. He saw me enter the booth area and immediately wanted to know "Why was I here?" He was obviously fearful that I was encroaching on another dealer's territory and even put in a call to my boss, Sam Cook, the owner of SVM to double check what was going on in California. Once reassured that all was in order, he relaxed. We enjoyed sharing the goals of our challenge with the other staff at the booth. We got to chat with familiar faces at the Bruno Independent Living display, as I have become very familiar with their product line over the years.

There were a number of wheelchair manufacturers there as well, with their latest and greatest products. I went looking for the TiLite booth and specifically the international salesperson Marty Ball, who is one of my mentors. There he was, like a postage stamp to a letter, always an expected part of all Ability Expos. He is always on the job, but finds time to continue racing at the age of 72.

We also had a chance to meet the ladies from the reality show "Push Girls." It aired on the Sundance channel. Then, sure as can be, we caught up with Mark Wellman, the "extreme athlete," with his rock wall. He's always eager to show how even though you have a disability you can still enjoy life, accomplish maybe some of what you did before your accident, and not be afraid to try anything. He was a mountain climber who in his haste to come down off a mountain, lost his footing and broke his back. However, he has not stopped living. He came back after rehab, became a parks ranger, and found a way back to climbing again with his disability. (Look more into his story at: www.NoLimitsTahoe.com.)

We highly recommend to anyone with a disability or in the rehabilitation industry that you go to one of these Ability Expos at any of the six locations. You will be amazed and enlightened about what is out there. It also keeps one updated on new equipment. The events at this race made it clear that being FLEXIBLE gave us a chance to attend one of six great Expos while meeting old friends and making new ones.

————

Possibilities

"If you believe you are born with all the smarts and gifts you'll ever have, you tend to approach life with a fixed mind-set. However, those who believe that their abilities can expand over time live with a growth mind-set and they're much more innovative."

— Dr. Marshall Goldsmith —

MARATHON #11
Cape May, New Jersey

"Open-Minded"

March 24, 2013
7:00 a.m.

The race director had said there have never been any racing wheel-chairs but there should be no problems except for a one-block stretch where the road was under construction. We immediately opted for an OPEN-MINDED attitude that would come into play race after race. Good thing, because the beach-front hotel was apparently opened only for this one weekend due to the race. It was quite outdated. We were given an actual metal key rather than a coded plastic credit card. The TV was so old that it had the rounded tube for projection. Also, there were not many eating establishments nearby, although we did eventually find one. However, our OPEN-MINDED outlook allowed us to enjoy the aroma of the ocean air, the sight of seagulls flying and the calming of waves crashing on the shoreline.

One shouldn't be afraid to reach out to anyone, for you never know who you might run into. As the saying by Will Rogers goes, "I never met a man that I didn't like."

This was not a huge race. It appeared to have been put together to bring some tourists to a town that is usually void of people at this time of year.

We would use an open-minded attitude numerous times during this race and why it was essential that we participate. We registered for this race only because it fit into our schedule. And it ended up being a great experience; we would love to go back and race again.

Grant reached out to tell the race director of our challenge and that we needed to take part in it for our New Jersey triumph. The director welcomed us and discussed the road construction options: we could either push through the rough gravel or wheel around the city block; the choice was ours. Traffic was very light at this time of year; he was not worried about which selection we would make. Because this was a point-to-point marathon along the Atlantic coastline, the race director was very kind to arrange an accessible bus to take our everyday chairs from the start to the finish and make it available to bring us back to the starting line near our hotel.

We felt we struck gold with the choice of our hotel; it was located on the beach and the price was a bargain. We then began to notice there were very few hotels open at this time of year. Upon our arrival, it was evident the hotel had not been renovated in quite a while. In the room, we wondered how many TV channels we could really get as there were no cables for satellite connection. Had we been one of the misfortunate to book a week-long vacation and have it rain the whole time, it would have been pure torture. We saved money, and it was the biggest room with two king-sized beds, but most guys don't sleep together, even in a king bed, so Aaron drew the short straw and took to the floor.

Grant and Aaron requested a late checkout because they were not flying out until the next day and were pleasantly surprised to hear the front desk clerk say, "They do not have anyone checking in and there will be nobody cleaning rooms until Monday. So feel free to stay as long as you want, with no additional fees." They left at 7:00 p.m. after a long afternoon nap, while I was driving back to Baltimore for my 8 o'clock flight to return to Kentucky so I could be back to work Monday morning.

Also scarce were the eating establishments open at this time of year. By asking the hotel staff for their recommendations, we found a great seafood restaurant. I don't often get the chance to smell that ocean air or hear the waves crashing along the shoreline, but to have such fresh seafood was a real treat. During the summer season, there would be a standing line at 11:00 p.m. waiting to get seated for their quality seafood. This was one of the special treats that helped us enjoy the challenge.

Just before the start of the Ocean Drive Marathon

The Ocean Drive Marathon in Cape May, New Jersey, was a great race even though the weather was brisk and damp, so close to the water. Cape May is at the southernmost tip of the state, where the Delaware Bay splits New Jersey and Delaware and opens up to the Atlantic Ocean. Hurricane Sandy had caused quite a ruckus in New Jersey, but luckily things were starting to get back together, thanks to the diligent efforts of the residents and business owners.

There seemed to be an air of excitement just prior to the start of the race; what the crowd lacked in size it did not lack in anticipation for the race to begin. We followed the road along the shoreline, inhaling the scent of the ocean and hearing the waves, although because of the bank and boardwalk, the ocean was not always visible to us. There were only a few turns and at one point we wheeled up on the boardwalk, which gave the race an extra highlight. As we were the only ones in the wheelchair division, we did push together.

With plenty of time in our head start, there would be no chance of a collision with any runners at the beginning. It was a relatively flat course. However, the wind would change direction at times; more often it was a headwind, so it helped Aaron and me to allow Grant to lead the way. Do you remember my mentioning how competitive Grant is? He said he would pull us the whole way, but sure enough when the first runner came up beside him, there he went! He took off, leaving us to deal with the wind on our own. He does not like to have any wheelchairs, hand-cycles, or runners come in ahead of him in any race.

With one exception, the course itself was well laid out and marked. Somehow Grant got detoured off the main course at about the 12-mile marker, but managed to get back on track about a half mile later. The culprit was probably the road construction issue mentioned earlier by the race director. I chose to go around, although Aaron chose to be the Marine … to tough it out and plow straight ahead. Perhaps that was why I finished before Aaron on this one.

The last mile was great for me because I caught a glimpse of what it could be like to live along the ocean, smelling the ocean breeze, seagulls overhead with familiar cry, but also having that calmness of waves crashing the shoreline. This was certainly an exhilarating end of the race.

The only downside was that it was the slowest mile I had done all year, just for the pleasure of taking in the sights before hurrying off to fly back to work on Monday.

Grant at the Finish Line

(We would like to give Special Thanks to Doug Rice of Split Second Racing for helping to organize the event. He can be contacted through www.SplitSecondRacing.net or by email at drice@raceforum.com.)

———

Race Results

675 runners, 3 wheelers and 1 hand-cyclist

1st (02:35:09) – Grant Berthiaume

2nd (02:56:35) – Paul Erway

3rd (03:07:55) – Aaron Roux

———

Behind the Scenes

Earlier in the story, I mentioned never knowing who you might meet.

Surprisingly, even though I took my time on the last mile to enjoy the ocean one last time, I finished the race ahead of Aaron. That had only happened once out of 11 races so far. We found the bus with our everyday chairs waiting near the finish. A gentleman who was just finished asked if he could get a ride with us back to the starting line. Because we were the only ones boarding and there were plenty of seats, we assured the bus driver that we did not mind and was glad to help if she would allow him to come along. So, as we were riding along, he asked how we did and if we race often together like this. We explained that this is number 11 of 50 we planned to do in a year, racing together in 50 states. He then asked why we had taken on such a big challenge. We replied that this was all about the Christopher & Dana Reeve Foundation.

He perked up and said, "Well, you must know Alexandra Reeve then, the daughter from Christopher's first marriage?"

We knew of his son whom he had with Dana, but never really looked into Christopher's earlier life. This gentleman said he went to college with Alexandra and actually saw her last week. He offered to forward our email addresses to her, thinking she might want to meet us at one of the races in her area.

Alexandra Reeve emailed us in a few days, saying that she had heard of our challenge and was very proud of us; however, she called us "crazy." We had heard that a lot already. She also said she had looked at our schedule of races and may have a chance to meet up with us at the Marine Corps Marathon in Washington, D.C.

What a chance! The one guy who shared a bus with us after
a marathon would end up introducing us to Alexandra? So always
be OPEN-MINDED, for you never know what great things
life has in store.

Possibilities

*"People become really quite remarkable when they start
thinking that they can do things. When they believe in
themselves, they have the first secret of success."*

— Norman Vincent Peale —

MARATHON #12
Knoxville, Tennessee

"Comradeship"

———

April 7, 2013
8:00 a.m.

I had been planning for this particular race since the idea of 50 marathons first came about. You see, the third member to go with Grant and I to Ōita, Japan, was Matthew Porterfield, whose home is in Knoxville. Matthew told us, "There have never been racing wheelchairs in this marathon before because of the hills. There have been hand-cycles, but never a racing chair."

That sounded like another challenge. Bring it on!

Grant and I sure were hoping that our COMRADESHIP we had formed with Matthew in Japan would cause Matthew to want to do the race with us. But that was as far as it would go with this race, as Matthew was already entered in another race in Charleston, South Carolina, the same weekend.

We all knew the Covenant Health Knoxville Marathon was going to be tough. There is nothing level in that part of the country as it is the foothills of the Smoky Mountains. You know it reminded me of home in

Pennsylvania where all the cows have one leg longer than the other due to the hills. Get the picture?

One positive thing about doing this race is that Tennessee was another one of the states in which we could get some support from Superior Van & Mobility. I would be on the job working while in the area because there is an office there. The city of Knoxville has a great rehab facility, the Patricia Neal Rehabilitation Center, named after the famous Academy Award-winning actress. They are fortunate to have Al Kaye coordinating their wheelchair sports as part of their Recreational Therapy Services. Al started a program through the rehab center to help folks who had experienced a life-changing event. He knew, like me, that life goes on after rehab. He created the Patricia Neal Innovative Recreational Cooperative, which is a perfect match for what we wanted to do with our racing adventure. The locals call it the IRC for short and it is an education and awareness program using recreation as a vehicle to motivate folks to succeed.

Matthew had directed me to Al, saying, "If you need anything done with wheelchair sports, you need this guy on your side."

He was right. I had set up a meeting with Al while on a marketing trip to the Knoxville early spring of 2011, where I told Al of the challenge. One of the first things Al said was: "You know there has never been a racing chair in this marathon because of the hills. You sure you don't want to use your hand-cycle for just this one marathon?"

Those of us who use racing wheelchairs are like a runner who uses sneakers — they are our way of competing in running races.

The hand-cycle is a whole other division, like bicyclists entering marathons. The hand-cycle looks like a recumbent bike where the rider is reclined back in a very low aerodynamic position. Plus, instead of one push rim on the wheel like a wheelchair, the cycles usually have 27 gears and your hands rotate handles like your feet pedal a bicycle. So, the hand-cycle can go a lot faster on the flat and downhill, but especially on the uphill, where the lowest gears can be utilized to just power up and over the hill which is a lot easier. As for us using racing wheelchairs, if the hill gets too steep, we can't push up for we may flip over. We either have to zigzag, or worse, we have to turn around and go up backwards at a much slower rate. There is much discussion nowadays about the possibility that hand-cycles should not be allowed in running races, but only in bike racing.

*Speaking with city officials before the marathon
at the University of Tennessee Stadium*

The main reason we wanted to do this marathon in this city is that the beneficiary of this race is Covenant Health, which is the parent company to the Patricia Neal Rehabilitation Center. I have seen the center's support and involvement in the community with patients like Matthew, who has competed in wheelchair racing on a state, national, and international level. There are numerous patients who have benefited from their program and the support from Al Kaye. I have seen other patients go through their program who Superior then helped get back on the road with vehicle modifications, and they all speak highly of Patricia Neal. I had an early start working with Al, who introduced me to Jason Altman, who is the Covenant Health Race Director. With their efforts, Knoxville became a great promoter of our challenge. They met with the three of us Wednesday before the race for a press conference. Present at this meeting were the Knoxville city mayor, Madeline Rogero, and the CEO of Covenant Health, Tony Spezia, in Neyland Stadium. Jason and Al were there as well.

Al reminded us that we could still do the race in hand-cycles if we wanted. We once again declined; our challenge has always been about the racing chairs. We also had a booth at the Fitness Expo to show off our racing wheelchairs and we made an hour-long presentation that was broadcast throughout the facility.

Before the kids' race with Tanner and Ethan

Two young guys, Tanner and Ethan, both about six years old, helped us understand a little more about ourselves while we were here in Tennessee. These two youngsters experienced spinal cord injuries before the age of three and were good buddies. (It is amazing how folks gravitate to support each other when put in similar circumstances.) These kids were boys through and through with laughter and exuberance that only comes from kids. Their parents wanted them to experience everything in life they could, so when they heard that we were coming to town, the parents wanted us to meet them. Their COMRADESHIP rubbed off on us too, as this was a reassurance of what we wanted to do with this challenge: Help bring awareness of wheelchair sports.

Al had Ethan and Tanner try all the different sports, even getting hand-cycles in their sixes so that they could try this sport. He had talked to the parents about letting the boys try the kids' race Saturday night because they had progressed so well. This would give them a taste of racing and he wanted us to be there to help kick off their very first race. It was a thrill for all of us to work with them. We observed that they interacted with each other as though they are just kids, not kids with a disability — beautiful reflection that people are people no matter what the circumstance. Their parents even moved to the same school district so the boys could have each other to rely on at the school, rather than being the only one using a wheelchair. The boys had worked on wheelchair sports and this provided their first experience of racing with about 1,000 other regular youths from the surrounding area. We met them at their race start to cheer them on and they were excited, as were their parents, to be the leaders of the pack and to finish in the Neyland Stadium on the 50-yard line, the sacred ground of the University of Tennessee Volunteers. This was a cool thing! Just one more reassurance of how this challenge was helping to bring an awareness of wheelchair sports to the Christopher & Dana Reeve Foundation.

I have to take a moment to mention another person we had the pleasure of meeting, Mike Fremont who was 91 years old. He was staying at the same hotel where we were and was in Knoxville to set the world record for the half marathon for 90 years old and over. He already held the

World Record for the full marathon and was going to run the full marathon, but when he found out there is no record for the half marathon, he chose to run the half at this race. Grant is 52 years old and I am 55. Mike Fremont gives us encouragement that we can possibly go on for another 35 years of future marathons. I had the honor to have my picture taken with him and his wife at the Health Expo.

With Mike Fremont, a world record holder for running a marathon at over 90 years of age. He is here to set a record for the half marathon.

Mr. Fremont was asked once if he diligently watches his times when working out.

"Why? I have no competition," he replied. "Do you know of anyone racing this distance who is over 90?"

He attributes his longevity to his vegan diet. I decided I should talk with my nephew, Kolomon Erway, about this when he runs with us in Baltimore later in the year. Kolomon is a long-time vegan who credits his diet for his ability to complete 100-mile races.

At the Starting Line for the Knoxville Marathon

RACE RESULTS

1st (02:30:21) – Grant Berthiaume

2nd (03:18:57) – Aaron Roux

3rd (03:48:37) – Paul Erway … not bad considering I flipped over on a steep hill on a bike trail that was part of the race course, I even still had dirt and grass stuck in the back of my helmet when crossing the finish line.

Behind the Scenes

As I mentioned before and will prove more times in this challenge, Grant is a beast. In every race, he has to go as fast as he can.

As if we did not have enough to do with a press conference Thursday afternoon, a Friday lunch-time presentation at Patricia Neal Rehabilitation, then speaking at the Health Expo at 3:00 p.m., Grant complicated the schedule even more by jumping into a vehicle to drive almost six hours to Mt. Pleasant, South Carolina, to race in the Cooper River Bridge Run on Saturday morning. Then he had to drive back another six hours to be back at Knoxville for racing in a full marathon on Sunday morning. Whew!

With Matthew Porterfield, who was with us in Oita Japan
when we first talked of 50 marathons

Our Knoxville resident friend, Matthew Porterfield who had joined us in Ōita, Japan, did not want to do the marathon with us because again, "No racing wheelchair has ever done this marathon with all of those hills." So you may say that it is contradictory to the theme of this chapter being named "COMRADESHIP," but the race results of Cooper River Bridge Run demonstrate that the spirit of comradeship was alive and well. Matthew was not aware of just how close he was ahead of Grant, but also, less than a minute behind Grant was Matt Davis from Bowling

Green, Kentucky, who was instrumental in helping plan our trip to Ōita. He was there with us and up to that point had raced in Ōita nine times before we went in 2010. So it was with their COMRADESHIP that Grant wanted to add this extra challenge to this weekend, and as he said "Well, I've done back-to-back marathons other weekends, this race is only a 10K." This guy is a beast and loves to "Put the hammer down."

***

Cooper River Bridge 10K
RACE RESULTS

April 6, 2013, Charleston, SC – 16 wheelchair racers

6th Matthew Porterfield – 0:29:49

7th Grant Berthiaume – 0:31:12

***

Possibilities

"Be around people who can keep your energy and inspiration high. While you can make progress alone, it's so much easier when you have support."
— Dr. Joe Vitale —

"Everybody is like a magnet. You attract to yourself reflections of that which you are. If you're friendly then everybody else seems to be friendly too."
— Dr. David Hawkins —

MARATHON #13
Adeline, Kansas

"Hospitality"

———

April 13, 2013
7:00 a.m.

This will be race #13 for the 50 Ability Marathons Team. It was reported to be a flat and fast course. That makes sense if you have ever driven or even talked to someone who has been through Kansas. The farther away you get from the eastern border, the flatter the land gets. And when it comes to racing wheelchairs, the less hills there are the faster the race will be.

For those not familiar with the flat plains of Kansas, Abilene is one of the original "Cow Towns" of the Midwest. Joseph McCoy, an entrepreneur from the late 1800s, promoted the transportation of longhorn cattle to the east coast. Cowboys would herd the cattle from Texas, north to Abilene, and along the Chisholm Trail, where they would be put on trains and shipped to the east coast cities. As you can imagine, Abilene was a tough and rowdy town, being the end destination for the cattle drive. Once the cowboys got their herd there, they got paid for the job. Of course, with a wad of cash in their pockets and no cattle to tend, most cowboys would tie one on at the local saloon before heading back to Texas. This made Abilene one of the wildest towns in the West and they needed a town marshal to help control the chaos. Two of the more notable marshals in this "Wild West" town were Tom "Bear River" Smith and Wild Bill Hickok.

Today, Abilene is known for Dwight D. Eisenhower. His family moved to Abilene from Denison, Texas, in 1892 and a young Dwight grew up there until attending and graduating West Point. Eisenhower went on to be a five-star general during World War II and later the 34th President of the United States. Dwight David Eisenhower wasn't born in Abilene, Kansas, nor did he die there. But the years he spent in the central Kansas town were among the most important of his life. We got a touch of history at this event where Abilene commemorates his life and legacy with the Dwight D. Eisenhower Presidential Library and Museum as well as the Eisenhower Marathon.

Visiting Eisenhower's High School

Yet, the description for the race focused back to the cattle days: "Runners at the Eisenhower Marathon and Half Marathon wind through the

territory south of Abilene that cattlemen followed when bringing their
herds to Abilene on the Chisholm Trail in the 1800s."

At the Starting Line for the Eisenhower Marathon

Luckily, the trail has been paved. Racers started in town by the
city's convention center and went a little more than two miles, made
a left into a park with paved roads for a loop, coming out and then
turning left to go farther out of town. On the return, we were turning
right back into the park for a loop again, coming out to go to the start
line for just completing the half marathon. For the full marathon, the
racers trekked the park four times. This was OK for a smaller marathon
like this because, for one, we kept seeing the same people on these roads
the whole time, but you were not sure if they were doing the half or full,
and if full, which part of the leg were they on. They really got to know
us and started clapping and cheering as we came by, so at the finish
we had a lot of runners come up to talk to us, thus allowing us to talk
about our challenge.

My hotel was a mile and a quarter from the starting line, so it was not much of a problem as I enjoyed it as a warm-up as I wheeled to the start that morning. But now going back, I found out, it was a lot of uphill — at least that is what it seemed like after 26.2 miles.

At the Finish Line

The temperature was just right for runners, as it was neither sunny nor raining. The best part was that the folks there made us feel at home. Everyone was great, from the time we rolled into the registration room of the convention center. Even the people at the restaurant, the police on the course, the crowd at the start and finish (who we got to see three times, the other runners some we may have seen maybe four times in the day) to the post-race. We experienced, enjoyed and embraced HOSPITALITY. Just good honest "Thanks for coming here," or, "Is there anything we can get for you?" or, "You guys must be having fun with all these races. Glad you came." They did not want us to leave hungry. They did not want us to feel unwelcome. We even got to meet some of the descendants of Dwight D. Eisenhower as well, wondering if he had the same hospitality in the White House.

RACE RESULTS

1st (02:01:24) – Grant Berthiaume

2nd (02:25:41) – Aaron Roux

3rd (02:48:53) – Paul Erway

Behind the Scenes

You always want to think your plans will go smoothly, but things happen that send everything into a tailspin and make it hard to get back on track. Such was the thought when the plane landed on time. I got to the car rental location way before rush hour starts to clog the highways, so no worries, right? I sat there third in line at the check-in counter and I felt I was getting a pretty good deal on this because the name of the company makes you think you are getting it for only a "dollar," but this ended up costing much more.

The person in front of me at the counter seemed to be having a problem because it was taking more than a half hour before he walked away with his contract. The line behind me is now huge and the lone attendant was not getting any help on this Friday afternoon. The rental I was to get turns out is a RAV 4, which is too small for a racing chair. So it takes a while for them to change to a large SUV, thus increasing the price immensely. So much for the deal!

I went to the area to pick out the vehicle and the only large SUV that I just paid for is locked, so I had to go back to the attendant, who said that it is reserved for someone, and there are no others that size. Why couldn't the attendant have told me that when he put it in the computer for that price that there were no full-size vehicles left? He took my paperwork to check it against the computer and came back saying he would help me find a vehicle. I'm thinking, what great customer service, right? We found a Jeep Cherokee into which my racing chair fit just fine and he said that it was the same price as the RAV 4, but I'd have to go back inside to get the price changed. I mentioned how long the line had gotten and the fact that it was rush hour, so I took the lump to choose to proceed with the higher price for a lesser vehicle just to get rolling.

With my racing chair loaded and my bag in the back, it was time for me to get in the driver's seat, but I messed up on my transfer and ended up on the ground with my everyday chair flipped back, all the while wondering what happened.

It was time to take a moment to think of how I was going to get out of this situation. The vehicle also happened to be at the end of the parking lot, so there was no one nearby to help. With built-up frustration, I flip the chair upright. Thank God I was graced with long arms so I could reach just the bottom edge of the steering wheel with one hand and the armrest of the driver's door to pull me up to the edge of the door sill. Then I grabbed higher and pulled harder to get my butt into the driver's seat. Now I only needed to get the everyday chair taken apart and fit it between my body and the steering wheel, placed into the SUV that already has a racing chair and luggage in the back, and then install the portable hand controls.

I was third in line at the gate where they checked paperwork to ensure I was the driver with the license and was taking the right vehicle. This should go smoothly, right? I was looking for that paperwork, which was nowhere around. I was next in line, still looking when I realized that the guy that I thought was good customer service had left my paperwork in his office at the other side of the parking garage and there were six cars behind me.

The checkout girl seemed nice and looked in the back by my bag to see if by chance it was there, which it wasn't, but she said she could print a new one. She went into her office, but couldn't find me in their system, so she called the front desk for help. Remember how busy they were? She was not getting any help from them either and after another 20 minutes of her going back and forth with their front desk and trying to reach the manager, drivers behind me were coming up to see what the holdup was and were voicing their frustrations. The checkout girl finally said that the front desk wanted me to go back inside with my driver's license to reprint the paperwork, even though she explained that I use a wheelchair and it would be difficult for me to do this. She also had to have all of the frustrated customers back up so I could pull out of the line. This was definitely going to be a happy Friday afternoon, don't you think?

I could not find the guy who had my paperwork so I had to go in. Now the line inside was down to just seven people, but this time there was a second person helping at the counter. There seemed to be a lot of people who were having problems with rentals from this company and again I ended up with another 30-minute wait for my turn. The good news was that now, at least, they could adjust the price to the original agreement. After all of this, the manager came out of his office and asked if he could be of service the moment the girl handed me my new contract with the right rental price. These are the times when one must take a deep breath, think of their very worst day and say, "If this was the worst thing that ever happened to me, I would be blessed." Sometimes you just have to let it go.

I have made it through two accidents and many operations, so I kept things in perspective. I turned to the manager and simply said, "I got it straightened out now, goodbye." No more, no less, and turned to go through loading again with the hope of not missing the transfer or losing the paperwork.

It was after rush hour when I finally got onto the highway, but it was also time to drive very fast to make it to the health expo and get the race number before they closed. It was hard to imagine when there would be time to grab a healthy dinner, then get pre-race food and drinks for in the morning, and prep the racing chair.

One would think my problems with this rental company were over, but returning the vehicle gave the company another chance to frustrate me. On Sunday, my hope was that it would be a little calmer. I even arrived at return rentals three hours before my flight, so I was not as rushed. I felt relaxed, only tired from the race itself. But that does not mean the rental staff were not rushed. They must be short on staff.

I pulled into the return lane as they instructed and as I started to remove my portable hand controls, the attendant asked for my paperwork, which, as you can imagine, I had placed within easy reach (a lesson learned). I unloaded my everyday chair and I seemed to take too long for their liking and they tried to move me along by what I think is good customer service: one of the attendants was unloading my racing chair. He also grabbed my luggage, which I instructed to place on my racing chair. He directed me to my airline as he jumped into the driver's seat to move the return rental.

It wasn't until I was at the TSA check-in that I realized my portable air pump was still in the rental. The attendant hadn't taken it out! It's my fault for not checking what I thought was a helpful attendant who actually did not help enough by looking further inside the vehicle. Yes, I do take some of the blame, but when I went back they told me the vehicle was taken off premises to be cleaned, but gave me the website with instructions of how I could make a claim to get lost items back. Simple, right?

The next day, I checked the website for returned items — nothing. So I made my claim of the exact item in the exact vehicle, VIN number and all, then waited. Checked again in few days and waited. Nothing. That was a new pump, which was used only three times before, so there was another $60 lost because of my choice to go with what I thought was an affordable rental car company.

Another Behind the Scenes

Grant and Aaron were flying into Kansas City before I did and we drove separate rental vehicles and stayed in different hotels. This was a benefit for them, but a disaster for me because the hotel I had was very low budget. We were trying to save where we could.

The hotel assured me that it was wheelchair accessible and I picked up the key, which brought memories of my hotel in Cape May, New Jersey, being outdated. This one was even worse. Wheeling down the sidewalk, I noticed that every door had a four-inch step, and sure enough there was one to my room as well. So much for meeting ADA codes! To be sure I had the right room, I doubled back to check.

The attendant confirms by saying, "Well, we can get you up that small step and once you get inside you should be OK?"

Great, how is that going to help at 5:00 a.m., getting ready for the race and then after? Going back to this room was not an easy task either, because the sidewalk was slightly angled and also became very steep to the parking lot, where I wheeled this time for a shorter straight shoot. After several tries from the parking lot, I found I was better off going back to the very beginning of the sidewalk once more and from the other end where it was easier because I had the luggage on my lap.

Once I opened the door, I had to throw the luggage to the inside first so I could pull myself over that four-inch step. No, this was not a wheelchair-accessible room just because one can pop themselves in. Accessible does not mean you only have to get your chair in; my chair could not fit into the bathroom, so once again I took a trip up to the front desk to see if they would pull the pins out of the door hinges to take the door off to see if I could at least get in the bathroom. There was no way of getting shower access, so I had to take a sponge bath after the race. There was NO HOSPITALITY at this hotel. However, the rest of the town truly did make up for it as this was a great experience for this marathon.

––––––––

Possibilities

"Motivation is what gets you started. Habit is what keeps you going."

— Jim Ryun —

MARATHON #14
Boston, Massachusetts

"Comprehend"

April 15, 2013
11:00 a.m.

Wheelchair racers finish first, so I was heading home, landing with a fellow passenger whose company sells running shoes and had a booth at the finish line. It wasn't until they landed to change planes that the passenger's cell phone began to beep constantly. I asked, "Did they tell you who won?" The response received made him fully understand the ability to "COMPREHEND."

"There was a bomb at the finish line."

I was stunned and tried to fathom what that must have been like for the racers, fans and this man whose company employees were in harm's way. Two days later, I was still grappling with thoughts about the whole experience — about the great high of completing the greatest race in the U.S. with our 14th race, then the tremendous low point, seeing the aftermath of the ones injured or dead and stories of heroes helping.

At 2:49 p.m. on Monday, April 15, 2013, the unthinkable occurred. A deed so horrendous that it will be remembered as one of those days that freeze in one's mind for all time, like JFK's assassination on

November 22, 1963, or the terrible destruction of September 11, 2001.
Every citizen of the USA — including the thousands of participants, and
the hundreds of thousands of friends and family who knew someone at
the Boston Marathon, can still pinpoint where they were at that particular moment. They remember what they thought and felt when hearing
or witnessing the atrocity of a terrorist attack at a marathon.

The reason I was homeward bound is threefold. First, as wheelchair
athletes, our start time is always earlier than the rest of the field; about 43
minutes at Boston. Second, we roll at a pretty quick pace, which means
that most of us will cross the finish line 10 to 40 minutes before the elite
male runners. With a start time of 9:17 a.m., I crossed the finish line 11
minutes before noon. That two-hour 32-minute total wasn't my swiftest,
but I was satisfied. Third, I had to be back at work the next morning. The
clock was ticking.

I had precious little time for a man with luggage, two wheelchairs,
additional security measures plus the normal logistics of hotel to airport
departure gate. I needed time to roll to the hotel, transfer from racing
chair to my regular chair, change clothes, collect my luggage, hail a cab,
endure the 15-minute drive to Logan, maneuver luggage and racing
chair to check-in, then maneuver through the daunting TSA Security
line before arriving at my gate with only 15 minutes to spare. Whew!
All of that did not seem so bad when everyone started clapping after
the Delta agent announced that I was the first Boston marathon
finisher at the gate.

I know where I was just four minutes before the bombing. My Delta
Airlines flight #1601 had just taken off from Boston's Logan Airport
en route to Louisville by way of Atlanta. The time? 2:45 p.m. In just
four minutes, while I was in the sky, the catastrophe now known as the
Boston Marathon bombings would occur. I wouldn't learn the details
until much later.

Pre-dawn … surreal … Monday, April 15, 2013 — this will be a very long day. Up at 4:00 a.m. An hour later, I push my racing chair from my hotel, which I chose because of its two-block proximity to the finish line, knowing that I had to rush to the airport post-marathon. My destination is the host hotel and the bus transport to the start area in Hopkinton. It's crazy how it was weirdly quiet. I was alone on the street underneath the banner of the actual finish line except for two police cars pointed in opposite directions. The officers wave. It would not be this still again. Certainly not at 2:49 p.m.

The flurry of day-long activities was about to begin. As the Boston Marathon start point is 26 miles away, the inevitable load, ride, and unload was the hectic prelude for what was to come.

With Dick and Rick Hoyt before the race

Before we boarded, TV crews filmed Team Hoyt, which is a story unto itself. Dick Hoyt was about to push Rick, his 51-year-old son, in their 30th Boston Marathon. Rick was disabled at birth due to cerebral palsy. They had completed about 1,100 events, including 70 at the marathon distance.

Hopkinton Athletes' Village was a local high school where athletes had access to a warm gym, restroom facilities, and energy drinks and bars. We could transfer into our chairs, burn off nervous energy, and talk with other racers before the event. We listened for race start announcements. As the qualifying maximum time for Boston was two hours and 30 minutes, I would be starting behind all of the wheelchair racers. I had qualified in 2:29:38, a scant 22 seconds for the good. As a bonus, I was directly in front of the Hoyts as they are in another division.

In the Hopkinton Athletes' Village

This would be my third Boston, where my best time was 2:06:17 in my very first year in 2004. But age, a second serious accident in 2006, and a strong headwind would slow me a bit. I don't remember this many uphills in previous tries, but the first few downhill miles are as fast as I remember, blazingly fast. With the finish line in sight, I was hurting big time as the last mile felt as if it was all uphill. I was extremely happy having completed one of the greatest athletic events in the world. Fourteen marathons down, 36 to go.

2:45 p.m. — Wheels up. It would be almost three hours before our plane touched down in Atlanta. The rest of the world knew what had transpired in those 165 minutes. We in the air did not, especially my seatmate and me, a man named Richie Woodworth, the president of Saucony Shoes. How did this odd couple get paired in First Class? I don't wear running shoes when racing and am almost always in coach.

As it turns out, the alignment of moon and stars was in harmony. Because boarding is a difficult transfer from my regular chair to a narrow contraption called an aisle chair, which can fit through very tight turns and navigate over a procession of bumps, I always board first. Once in a while, a First Class seat is available, and, in this case, after some passenger politely agreed to change seats, I was assigned to 1C in the front row. Soon, Richie Woodworth joined me, and as he was stepping over me to get to the window seat I noticed his running shoes.

"Are you a runner or do you just like really nice running shoes?" I asked.

"I'm the President of Saucony Running Shoes, Richie Woodworth."

We talked about Boston, my three-marathon history there and, of course, our 50 Marathon Challenge. I talked about the CDRF efforts to support people with spinal cord injuries and threw in a plug for possible sponsorship. We were both tired, me from my 26.2 and he from a long week of marketing, entertaining distributors, and hosting the Saucony Expo exhibit. We became quiet and I drifted off to intermittent sleep.

We landed at 5:30 p.m. Cell phones were activated. Richie's went crazy with a lot of dinging and buzzing. Mine followed suit shortly thereafter. His whole demeanor quickly changed. He was very quiet; reading and texting.

"Did they tell you who won?" I asked.

"There was a bomb at the finish line."

I was stunned in disbelief and confusion.

The passengers started to deplane. Word of the bombing spread like wildfire. Richie stayed in place, concentrating on his phone. He said that Saucony had a booth at the finish line. I could not imagine his fear and dread. My 26 emails, 13 texts and nine voicemails were all from family and friends concerned about my well-being. He was distraught, not fully knowing the fate of his employees and team. I could not imagine what he must have been going through.

He left his seat at the next line gap stating that he needed to book a plane back to Boston and find a secure place to make some calls. He cordially said goodbye and turned to say, "Good luck in your races."

A few days later I learned from a Saucony vice president, after my email inquiry, that no company employees were hurt. He very personally thanked me for my concern.

Atlanta — I had more than three hours for a layover before my flight to Louisville would depart. My head was buzzing with the euphoria of finishing my 14th marathon of 2013, the joy of racing Boston again, but then there was the down side emotions of the event. It was the fear of what I would learn in the coming days.

The aftermath of 2:49 p.m. on that day filled me with sadness, anger, and confusion. The stories of those not able to finish, some so very close, filled me with compassion. All were tired. Many had no money for a cab, no cell phone, no knowledge of what had occurred, at least early on. Some walked side streets looking for food, water, land lines and transport.

Accounts of what happened that day sounded like an end-of-the-world science fiction movie. To some, that is exactly what it was.

Epilogue – This story was about time and timing, both good and bad. It was about a vacuum of knowledge. It was about my luck. And, it was about wheelchairs. If I hadn't qualified by 22 seconds, I would not have been in Boston. If I finished 10 or 15 minutes later, my plane would have left without me or I'd be stuck at my hotel for hours. If I was a runner, I would have been somewhere on the course, or worse. Receiving the news there, over several hours, would have affected me differently.

Processing the incomplete story in Atlanta and en route to Louisville felt unreal and so difficult to comprehend. Even the atmosphere in the airport. Fellow travelers were saddened and subdued.

As time passed, we would learn that many of the injured lost limbs or suffered spinal damage. Wheelchairs helped them recover or transition. Some now use their arms to ambulate instead of their legs. Their recoveries have been heroic. Time has passed and they thrive. Thrive! The Boston Strong resiliency is ever present.

Remembering Boston

I will never again look at the Boston Marathon as before. I've grown from the experience and my return is a certainty. This story was short on actual marathon descriptions but they would have paled with reality.

RACE RESULTS

Grant and Aaron did not enter in time for Boston. They planned to try to pick up the Old Colony Marathon in Springfield, Massachusetts in late May.

Overall 49/52, Division 39/41 (02:32:20) – Paul Erway

Behind the Scenes

The year was 1987 and my coach had talked me into doing my very first marathon. Philadelphia was not too far away, as I lived near Harrisburg, Pennsylvania, at the time. The course looked pretty flat and I had raced on some of those roads before. After that first race, I did not shower for three days because my arms hurt so much that I could not transfer into the shower. I swore I would never ever do another marathon. However, with better training, I was prevailed upon to enter two more marathons. Same result, each time saying, "This is the very last, I will never ever do a marathon again."

I still had this racing bug but for shorter races and eventually I qualified for the developmental team for track racing, concentrating on the 100-meter through to the 1,500-meter. I traveled to the World Championships in 1990 in Assen, Holland.

What an experience! It was my first time overseas, first international competition, and so much more. Then the team coaches informed me that the USA had too many competitors in the 1,500-meter race. Because I had the slower time, they would have to take me out of that event.

But then later on they asked, "Would you want to now do the marathon? It's not limited in the number of entries."

For the past couple of years, I had been honing my training to sprints, but I had spent two weeks over there and had been on the track all of three and a half laps.

"Yes, put me in," I replied, thinking that I could at least get to see some of the countryside of Holland. I could have a nice long rest on the flight home.

I did the marathon in 2:02:54 ... a full hour faster than the previous marathons, cutting my time by a third. Training for sprints taught me the faster I raced, the less energy I expended since I wasn't pushing as long. I wasn't as tired. And I felt great the next day. I was thinking, "That wasn't so bad!"

With new insight on my training, I could do these distances.

The next two years, I concentrated on the sprints because I wanted to make the Paralympics in 1992.

There we were, in Salt Lake City, Utah, for the Nationals where they were to choose the Paralympic team and this little guy shows up. He was at Junior Nationals the week before in Florida. He did so well they brought him to the Adult Nationals. And he beat me!

I felt like I was too old to compete with the young and fast; I kind of gave up racing because I lost my dream of making the Paralympics.

In the spring of 2003, I was talking to Marty Ball, one of the greatest wheelchair racers, who had been inducted into the Hall of Fame of Wheelchair Racing. Because of him we have a Masters Division and now a Grand Masters Division for wheelchair racers. He told me that before I give up on racing, I have to do the Boston Marathon to experience the greatest race in America. But you don't just pay an entry and jump in this race. You have to qualify. You have to do another marathon fast enough to get you in ... meaning I have to start training again.

In the fall of 2003, I qualified at the Columbus, Ohio, Marathon, and in the spring of 2004, I was racing in Boston with a mile to go, just enjoying the experience ... just like Marty said I should. Then with just a mile to go in what I think will be my last marathon ever, "POW!" I get a flat. But I look down and see how fast I have done it in so far and I don't care if it ruins my disc wheel. I just crank out that last mile finishing in 2:04:17.

Marty got me hooked on racing again. That is what mentors do, isn't it? They find ways to keep pushing you to bigger goals. In my case, it was getting back into racing. This is why the Boston Marathon holds a special place in my heart. Through this lesson I learned to COMPREHEND how important mentors can be. It is my hope that I, too, can make a difference in someone else's life.

Possibilities

"When something bad happens you have three choices, you can let it define you, let it destroy you, or you can let it strengthen you."

— Dr. Seuss —

EPILOGUE

I'll always remember the day of the 14th marathon in the 50-Marathons Challenge, and it seems a fitting place to end this first book. I had just finished one of the greatest marathons in the United States, and knew I accomplished a great goal. I was relaxing on the two-hour plane ride, enjoying the accomplishment. But my emotions changed in an instant when the plane landed, I turned on my phone and found the news of something as tragic as death. The cruel game of life.

In one moment, I felt so good about myself; I was so high with excitement. Then totally unexpectedly I was thrown back down so low. For a time, I questioned if this is really worth all the effort.

President Obama said on the day of the Boston Marathon bombing, "I'm here today on behalf of the American people with a simple message: Every one of us has been touched by this attack on your beloved city. Every one of us stands with you."

Generally, we are reaching for something, directed toward knowing that along the way we will have situations come up that test us. Everyone, in his or her life, faces tests. These tests make for markers in our lives. They are gauges of how we are doing, to see if we can take on more or to go further in life. We have to look in the mirror to see what we are made of, to push through, to reach within ourselves toward accomplishing what we started out to achieve.

When I made it to the World Championships, for instance, it was magnificent. But they were nonetheless a kind of marker for me to make the Paralympics. The games afford a setting for a test, with the advantage that the results come straightaway. It comes with no ifs, ands, or buts. They challenge you to face your inner voices, to see your insecurities, confront the human emotion of fear, of not performing to your best ability. The games are as in life: I can give in, or I can fight. I have the choice. Perhaps I prevail, maybe not, but if I am supposed to lose today, then let me be brave in the attempt of trying. Because I am going to try no matter what. Isn't that what we should be doing in the game of life?

Thus the games are an extension of what we are reaching for and dreams each of us have in all areas of life itself. The winning itself can mean something very different. It means the effort, emotion, and the sportsmanship to never give up, the never-say-die mentality.

Making the World Championships but then not making the Paralympics seemed a tremendous setback after a great feat. But was it? This may have been the situation the past two times of me racing in the Boston Marathon in 2004 and 2010. I had set the goal to get there with diligent training months in advance, and planned to be fast enough at a race that would get me qualified toward even be able to register for the race. Then once I crossed the finish line of the greatest marathon, I realized I wanted to come back; I was immediately driven by an inner force to do better, to improve on myself and my personal record time. But for those races, I was done. It's an interesting enigma to feel most motivated to keep rolling when the finish line is behind you.

But for me, there would always be more starting lines and more finish lines. Even in the aftermath of the complex and mixed emotions following the bombing at the Boston Marathon, I was able to feel hopeful because this wasn't the only race I had planned for the year. It was race #14 of 50. It was an important race, but it was not the end. We had specifically planned Boston into our larger scheme, knowing it was a must-not-miss marathon. Because the race turned so dark, I was left wondering if I should just pull out of the whole challenge. Or do I, as in past setbacks, pick myself back up again?

The answer was always clear. It was time to keep rolling. To pick myself back up again. For in just five days, I needed to be at the starting line of another marathon. The plan was 50 marathons, in 50 states. Boston was just one of those tests that will happen to us. Yes, I completed it, but mentally I had been tested to see if I have in me the ability to come back. Could I, in just four short days, pull my equipment together, pack my clothes, make the trip through TSA at the airport, all over again? Is this really worth the effort?

I think so. And I hope that you as readers (and perhaps racers yourself) think so too. Sport can seem awfully trivial. Yet there is something about sport. It speaks to the best in each of us, to our hopes and dreams, to our vision of a better world. We honor sacrifice and carry forward the struggle, each of us in our own way.

The 50 marathons were important to me, and also to Grant and Aaron. And by writing about what we experienced and learned, it's my hope that they will become important to you. Through our journey, you may recognize the reasoning behind making grand plans. It's powerful to have something to reach for — a proverbial prize that you want so badly that you keep driving to achieve it. Once completed, you take a moment to reflect on your accomplishment. You realize then something surprising and miraculous: "If I can do this, then what is the next level, what possibilities are that I need/want to gain?"

The worst of the bad setbacks that you may have had? You stick them in the dark recesses at the back of your mind, and save them for when you start to have another test. You reflect upon having made it through that bad setback, knowing you can make it through this one. Believe "I have the strength to make it."

Extreme challenges like the 50/50/50 offer so many moments when it would be so easy to quit. That's why you have to find a bigger reason of WHY. Create audacious goals with a bigger reason than you. When you have others you have to help, you can't quit. For me, Grant and Aaron, this challenge for us was about helping other men, women and children who had experienced spinal cord injuries. The bigger goal made us stronger. And we used the problems we encountered to gain wisdom in ways that would strengthen us personally and collectively.

Moreover, by sharing with you, the reader, these struggles, setbacks, and strife we faced through this challenge, you, too, may gain strength from us. You may not use a wheelchair, but knowing what we went through and that we have made it this far, may make a difference for you. And we believe that your achievements in spite of or after adversity will allow you to help other people too. Keep rolling.

I remember being a child of five years old, and my father telling me, "Get back on the horse." He knew the lessons I would learn from this simple action — he knew I'd develop dedication and courage. By getting back on, I am overcoming my fear, taking control, and, Oh, what a ride I will have when I do.

So, here I am at the end of my first book and my 14th "50 Abilities" marathon. I have the plane tickets, my hotel room is reserved, and I am registered for the Salt Lake City Marathon. Time to get back in the saddle. The only question is will the Salt Lake City Marathon cancel their event because of the catastrophe in Boston?

And then I hear in my heart what we've been hearing ringing through the air and on the airwaves, "Boston Strong, Boston Strong ..." Indeed.

———

Possibilities

"You gain strength, courage, and confidence by every experience in which you really stop to look fear in the face. You are able to say to yourself, 'I have lived through this horror. I can take the next thing that comes along.'"

— Eleanor Roosevelt —

Don't miss the rest of the stories from Paul, Grant and Aaron's final 36 marathons, recounted in the second and third books in the 3-book series, due out in 2018.

———

Be inspired. Be strong.
Be full of unlimited possibilities.

RESOURCES

Throughout this book, mention has been made of many wonderful organizations and brands. As a courtesy to readers who may be interested in learning more, the author has compiled the following selective list.

Chapter 1

University Rehabilitation Center
www.ummchealth.com/rehabilitation

The Mississippi Blues Marathon
www.msbluesmarathon.com

Chapter 2

TIRR Memorial Hermann Rehabilitation Center
www.memorialhermann.org

*Thank you to **Rhonda Abbott**, PT Director of Therapy Services and Director of Clinical Programs, and **Jenny Gomez**, Recreational Therapy and Adaptive Sports.*

The Chevron Houston Marathon
www.chevronhoustonmarathon.com

Ryan Terry (owner), Bicycle World of Houston
www.bicycleworldofhouston.com

———

Chapter 3

Jo Crawford, CTRS, MSL
www.thebarrow.org

The Rock 'N' Roll Arizona Marathon
www.runrocknroll.com/arizona

———

Chapter 4

Miami Physical Therapy
www.miamipta.com

Thank you to **James Fenton***, DPT, and to*
Miriam Guanche*, MSPT Clinical Director.*

Sabrina Cohen Foundation
www.sabrinacohenfoundation.org

Harry R. Horgan, COE, Shake-A-Leg Miami
www.shakealegmiami.org

Jim Albert, Mobility Works
www.automobilitysales.com

The Miami Marathon
www.themiamimarathon.com

———

Chapter 5

The Myrtle Beach Marathon
www.mbmarathon.com

———

Chapter 6

HealthSouth Lakeshore Rehabilitation Hospital
www.healthsouthlakeshorerehab.com

*Thank you to **Paula Stewart**, M.D., Medical Director,
and **Jinnie Lacey**, RN, Rehabilitation Liaison.*

The Lakeshore Foundation
www.lakeshore.org

The Birmingham Mercedes-Benz Marathon
www.mercedesmarathon.com

*Thank you to **Jill Jowers Edwards**, Assistant Race Director.*

Chapter 7

Baton Rouge Rehabilitation Hospital
www.brrehab.com.

*Thank you to **Roxane Bingham**, Rehabilitation Liaison.*

Touro Rehabilitation Center
www.touro.com/rehab

*Thank you to **Maureen Herring**, M.Ed.,
LOTR Rehabilitation Services Educator.*

Sam & Kathy Cook (owners), Superior Van
www.superiorvan.com

The Rock 'N' Roll New Orleans Marathon
www.runrocknroll.com/new-orleans

Chapter 8

The Albany Marathon
www.albanymarathon.com

HealthSouth Rehabilitation Hospital
www.healthsouth.com

Chapter 9

The Little Rock Marathon
www.littlerockmarathon.com

Chapter 10

Janne P. Kouri, President and Founder, Next Step Fitness
www.nextstepfitness.org

The Los Angeles Marathon
www.lamarathon.com

*Thank you to **Laura and Jairo Rivera**,
Directors of Wheelchair Division.*

Chapter 11

The Ocean Drive Marathon
www.odmarathon.org

Doug Rice, Split-Second Racing
www.splitsecondracing.net

———

Chapter 12

Patricia Neal Rehabilitation Center
www.patneal.org

*Thank you to **Al Kaye**, M.S., CTRS Clinical Specialist,
Director of Adaptive Sports Program.*

The Knoxville Marathon
www.knoxvillemarathon.com

*Thank you to **Jason Altman**, Race Director.*

Sam and Kathy Cook (owners), Superior Van
www.superiorvan.com

———

Chapter 13

The Eisenhower Marathon
www.eisenhowermarathon.com

———

Chapter 14

The Boston Athletic Association
www.baa.org

*Thank you to **Kara McDonald**,
Race Registration Coordinator, 117th Boston Marathon.*

EQUIPMENT AND
OTHER ITEMS USED

In 1988, Sportaid was the first company of its kind. Sportaid has grown
from a supplier of racing tires, wheelchairs, racing suits, and other
racing-related equipment to a supplier of everyday wheelchairs, wheelchair cushions, medical supplies, urological supplies, and daily living aids.
Medaid, a division of Sportaid, assists its customers in getting third-party
reimbursement. In 1996, they launched their website and became the
first supplier of wheelchairs and related products on the internet. It
was in 1990 when I was in a room with six other athletes at the World
Championships in Assen, Holland, that I really got to know Jimmy
Green, Founder of Sportaid, and have been using their services and products ever since. (www.sportaid.com, 800-743-7203)

- My everyday chair is a TiLite ZR Rigid Titanium Wheelchair
  (www.sportaid.com/tilite-aero-t.html).

- My cushion is the ROHO Hybrid Elite Dual Compartment
  Wheelchair Cushion (www.sportaid.com/ROHO-Hybrid-Elite-
  Wheelchair-Cushion.html).

- I do have two set of wheels, one for every day and Aluminum
  Billet Wheels for speaking engagements (www.sportaid.com/
  spintek-phoenix-aluminum-billet-wheels.html). I use 700c x 19mm

Continental Podium TT Tire (195g) for racing because it is up to 220 PSI and typically weight of over 200 lbs., thus giving me the best ride (www.sportaid.com/encore-deluxe-constriction.html).

My many thanks to Permobile for their influence in shaping seating and mobility solutions. They are the main brand for those two products, a brand that is asked for by name, known for quality and trusted by therapists, prescribers, dealers and consumers to be the best.

- Coloplast Urological & Catheter Supplies (www.sportaid. com/mentor/)

Made in USA - Kendallville, IN
43184_9780999149133
02.06.2023 1334